"COMPASSIONATE AND [...] will help ensure a far bette[r ...] and your dog than sheer lea[...] domination."—Dr. Michael W. Fox, Scientific Director, The Humane Society of the U.S.

An invisible leash is the bond between owner and pet, based on knowledge, confidence, understanding, patience, and—above all—love. Dr. Myrna M. Milani shows you how to forge and develop this bond and helps you to understand: which dog will be the friendliest of a litter or the most aggressive; why consistency in training is important; the touch that brings out the best in your dog; the important relationship between food and behavior; how you can help your older dog's failing senses; and the six most important steps for solving any problem with your dog.

THE INVISIBLE LEASH

"Reasoned and insightful.... Milani knows that the only solution to the neuroses of dog owners is education... calmly presented facts in common-sense lingo ... Milani judges dogs, and humans, with a great heart."
—Job Michael Evans, *Dog Fancy*

DR. MYRNA M. MILANI is a practicing veterinarian and teacher, specializing in the care, training, and treatment of small animals. She is a past president of the New Hampshire Veterinary Medical Association and author of *The Weekend Dog*, available in a Signet edition. Dr. Milani lives in Fitzwilliam, New Hampshire, with her husband, two dogs, and a cat.

THE INVISIBLE LEASH

A BETTER WAY TO COMMUNICATE WITH YOUR DOG

MYRNA M. MILANI, D.V.M.

A SIGNET BOOK

NEW AMERICAN LIBRARY

A DIVISION OF PENGUIN BOOKS USA INC., NEW YORK
PUBLISHED IN CANADA BY
PENGUIN BOOKS CANADA LIMITED, MARKHAM, ONTARIO

Note to the Reader

The ideas, procedures, and suggestions contained in this book are not intended as a substitute for consulting with your veterinarian. Matters regarding the health of your dog require medical supervision.

NAL BOOKS ARE AVAILABLE AT QUANTITY DISCOUNTS WHEN USED TO PROMOTE PRODUCTS OR SERVICES. FOR INFORMATION PLEASE WRITE TO PREMIUM MARKETING DIVISION, NEW AMERICAN LIBRARY, 1633 BROADWAY, NEW YORK, NEW YORK 10019.

A hardcover edition of *The Invisible Leash* was published by New American Library and simultaneously in Canada by The New American Library of Canada Limited.

 SIGNET TRADEMARK REG. U.S. PAT. OFF. AND FOREIGN COUNTRIES
REGISTERED TRADEMARK–MARCA REGISTRADA
HECHO EN WINNIPEG, CANADA

SIGNET, SIGNET CLASSIC, MENTOR, ONYX, PLUME, MERIDIAN AND NAL BOOKS are published by New American Library, a division of Penguin Books USA Inc., 1633 Broadway, New York, New York 10019

First Signet Printing, December, 1986

3   4   5   6   7   8   9

PRINTED IN CANADA

To Brian—
The best communicator, in every sense of the word

Acknowledgments

The Invisible Leash could not have been written without the help of these very special people:

Cindy Kane, who planted the original seed;

Michael Snell, who helped it grow;

Nancy Butcher, who took over midstream; and

Marjorie Zerbel who typed whenever asked and cheered me up on numerous occasions

Contents

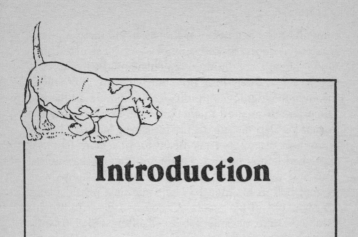

Introduction

Last winter my old dog Dufie died. Despite the fact that as a veterinarian I'd helped hundreds of dog owners cope with the deaths of beloved pets, I felt as if I'd lost a member of my family. Like all dog owners, I thought my dog was extraordinary and our bond with each other was special and unique. Sure, Dufie was no more than your basic generic brown American dog, the kind of mongrel whose lineage contains every breed from beagle to shepherd; but no other dog looked like him, and no other dog wagged its tail quite the same way when I talked to it.

In ten years of small animal practice I treated and talked to a lot of dogs, but never a dog like Dufie. Although he never displayed the keen intelligence of a Doberman or the manners of a well-trained poodle, he had his own brand of wisdom and warmth. How well I remember the agonies of trying to train him as a pup! I barricaded doors, locked cabinets, and constructed anti-Dufie pyramids of dining room chairs on the living room couch, all to keep him from misbehaving. But either through maddening stupidity or incredible brilliance, Dufie always seemed to *choose* not to behave badly the instant I'd take these extreme measures. The day I came home and discovered my beautiful Schefflera (another cherished family member) dismembered on the kitchen floor and Dufie racing joyfully through the house with its root ball in his mouth, I put my most prized plants up high, out of his reach. A soon as I went to all this trouble, Dufie became totally disinterested in plants, even easily accessible ones.

No, Dufie was no ordinary dog. He'd play in cardboard boxes for hours; but if I picked one up to move it out of the way, he'd go berserk with fear, urinating, emptying his anal glands, and scurrying for cover as if he'd never seen such a horrible object before. "What a dufus!" we'd say. And the name stuck.

Whenever he barked too much, or lifted his leg on the center post in the basement, I yelled at him. If he whined at faraway skunks at three in the morning, I assured him nothing was there. I shared my lunch with him and screamed at him when he stole food off the counter. In short, in the twelve years Dufie and I were together we communicated in every way from sound, sight, smell, taste, and touch to that special sharing called love. In such a way we created a bond, an invisible leash that held us together in a very special manner.

Having shared so much together, I felt his death as I would that of a dear friend and companion. I put Dufie to sleep in accord with the philosophy I worked out as I watched him age and deteriorate physically until slippery hardwood floors, narrow staircases, and the icy New England winter became treacherous foes of his weakening eyesight and arthritic hips. Having approached such mundane problems as barking, car chasing, house soiling, and begging with my growing understanding of a dog's senses, I resolved to approach his death with an understanding of that ultrasense called love. I wanted our final moments together to be our deepest communication ever. When the day came that I felt I could no longer outweigh his discomfort with my own fears of separation and death, I chose to put Dufie down myself as we sat together on the warm tile hearth that had become his favorite spot.

When I first tried to give him the injection, my trembling hand missed the vein, but Dufie didn't flinch or pull away. He trusted my touch, the sound of my voice, the familiar smell of my baggy old sweater. I switched the syringe to his other front leg and this time, I didn't miss. I cradled his paw in my hand and gazed into his old brown eyes as I had so many hundreds of times when he gently batted me for attention. Somehow I feel Dufie knew exactly what I was doing and why. Our years together had built such a strong bond of communication we both understood our final moment was far more than the sum total of the experiences we had shared. I doubt there's any recording device capable of following our exchange of canine and human thoughts and emotions, the waves of ineffable interspecies communication racing across the imperceptible bridge between us in those final seconds.

Dufie is buried at the highest point in the back field because, as my sons put it, "He's been with us the longest and should have the best view." There are pine boughs in the bottom of his grave to keep him dry and others on top to keep him warm. My youngest, Dan, thought we should bury his bowl with him. Even then, we somehow still believed Dufie could see, feel, smell, hear, and taste. Maybe Dufie has gone romping off into some sunny canine afterlife or maybe not; but he's still with us because the communication we shared is still very much alive.

What makes a good communicator? What enables a dog to convey its feelings and needs to people? How do people convey their needs and feelings to their dogs? Ask any dog owner, from cantankerous Hank down the street with his ill-mannered, one-eyed black Lab to Lassie's trainer, and you'll quickly learn that, regardless of a dog's breed or intelligence, every loving owner can tell when his or her dog is happy, bored, fearful, or not feeling well. The owners' noses tell them the instant they open the door if their dogs have messed in the house; and similarly, the dogs' noses cover every inch of their owners' clothing to find out where they have been and what interesting people or animals they've encountered. Special barks warn "Someone's coming!" Sensitive ears pick up the sound of Johnny measuring out kibble a mile away. Just as human beings communicate with one another using their five senses (and a sixth some call love), owners and their animals employ the full range of sensations creating an invisible leash that binds them together. Only when we expect our dogs to respond to sensations the same way we do does the communication break down and create problems.

How do we link up with a species whose view of reality is often so different from our own? Over the years, Dufie and my clients and patients have taught me a lot about the beauty and richness of interspecies communication, especially that the quality of that communication depends on both species paying close attention to the other's unique use of the senses. The two species speak different languages, and each must master the other's form of communication for love to flourish. When a shy pet urinates on door frames and draperies to mark or protect the property, an insensitive owner might misinterpret the message as one of meanness and spite. If that owner swats the dog to teach it not to do such a horrible thing, abuse, not communication, occurs. Any form of touch immediately tells a dog to defend itself in one of three ways: to freeze, fight, or flee; so rather than that swat communicating the owner's "Don't urinate there!" the message the dog receives elicits one of the three defensive responses. Furthermore, even these natural canine responses are misinterpreted. The dog who freezes is a coward; the fighter wins a one-way ticket to the vet's to be put down for viciousness; the dog that flees will get another swat when (and if) it returns. In short, a dog's natural response to sensation is not the same as ours. No wonder so many owners have trouble solving problems with their dogs.

Once our increased awareness of how human and canine communication are similar and different enables us to link up with our pets, we can use this bond to enrich our relationships. Ideally, it would be nice to begin establishing that bond the day Percy enters our lives as a lovable pup; that way we can prevent a lot of problems. However, linking up with an older animal is not without its own special rewards. In addition to expanding the owner's appreciation of the dog's natural methods of communication, the bond can also provide alternative solutions to many common problems that often undermine even the most loving relationship.

How can we use our knowledge of communication to

solve problems? Like using a nylon or leather leash, using the invisible leash of communication to guide or alter behavior is a lot easier if we consistently use the same process. In the pages ahead we'll develop a simple six-step problem-solving procedure that can be used on a wide variety of communication and behavioral problems. The first step in this process is to recognize the existing situation as normal, regardless how horrible the behavior or our feelings about it might be. Does this sound impossible? Well, it's not really that difficult and once you learn how to do it, it can save you a lot of time. Defining the problem is another step that helps simplify problem solving. Many times owners get poor responses to their efforts because they haven't taken the time to figure out what the real problem is. Yelling at Leopold for soiling the rug isn't going to work if Leopold messes because he's scared to death of the sound of your neighbor's motorcycle and urinates every time he hears it. Similarly, selecting a solution without collecting information is little more than guessing and often based on fiction or convention rather than your or your dog's needs. Such solutions are often doomed from the start. Once we define the problem, collect information, and select and implement the solution, we'll learn how to evaluate our results. Is it working? Should we try something else or alter our approach? Should we keep going another month?

By using this process owners can see how even complex problems with all sorts of emotional overtones ("George thinks Serena has a problem, but I think she's perfect") can be separated into simple and manageable parts. In each step we examine not only what the dog is communicating, but what we are communicating to the dog. We learn there are dog problems and there are people problems, but most of them are a little bit of both.

The Invisible Leash explores all the different ways people and dogs communicate. Each chapter examines typical puppy and adult behavior as well as that associated with particular breeds and breed types. By the end of the book, you'll not only have a better understanding of how you and your dog communicate, you'll be able to use that increased understanding to develop a more mutually rewarding relationship with your pet. The invisible leash is that special magic which uniquely bonds an owner and an animal. It isn't something you either have or you don't. It's something the two of you recognize together, something that grows as the two of you grow.

After I put Dufie to sleep, I had to drive from my New Hampshire home to Boston shortly after sunrise. The sky was unusually beautiful, turbulent gray clouds mingled with bright patches of sunlit blue, and Dufie was very much on my mind. Even though I knew I'd done the right thing, I wanted some reassurance, some sign. And I got one—a magnificent rainbow. Scientists would say it's common to see rainbows on such occasions, but I'll always remember that special one because at the time it seemed like a bridge, the invisible leash, between two old friends, evidence that good relationships are timeless.

Let's journey together through the simple and ordinary mechanisms all people and animals possess, those physical, mental, and emotional capacities that enable us to communicate on many levels. Along the way you'll encounter some people and dogs who are as extraordinary as you and your pets.

Part I

Understanding the Invisible Leash

Making Sense of Interspecies Communication

We tend to regard spoken or written words as the most reliable forms of communication, even though we simultaneously recognize most of the world's problems stem from our inability to fully master these forms. Whether the problem is a lovers' quarrel, a war, or a misbehaving dog, we can usually trace the problem to the fact that the parties involved (including the dog) have not conveyed their needs to each other in a mutually understandable and acceptable way.

So how can people who fail to communicate perfectly with one another ever hope to communicate with another species? Well, perfect communication may be impossible in this imperfect world, but we can come closer to achieving it as we learn to use *all* of our senses to send and receive messages instead of relying on just one or two.

Interspecies Communication

Although poets and diplomats must rely on a limited vocabulary of written and spoken words, dog owners can use sound, sight, smell, taste, touch, and that most perfect sixth sense, love. To be sure, the senses play a role in most human communication. Someone's bad breath or delicate perfume, bone-crushing or gentle handshake, or loud or soft voice can influence our responses; but the fact remains that most people consider these more subtle aspects of communication as secondary. As we begin to explore the world of interspecies communication, we must learn to view the senses as primary aspects of communication because they, more than words, build good relationships between people and their pets. Dogs do "verbalize" to each other via barks, whines, and growls, and many dog owners believe they can communicate with their pets by imitating these sounds. By the same token, many owners insist their dogs understand every word they say, Southern drawl, New England twang and all.

Although such verbal communication does play a role in our relationship with our pets, it doesn't play the only, or even the most important one. Does your dog wag its tail or cuddle closer when you pet it? Does it bounce with joy when you open a can of dog food? Have you watched it, oblivious to your shouts, dash off, lured by the scent of another animal? Before we tackle problems caused by miscommunication with our dogs, we must understand how their senses work, and how they compare with our own.

Lend Me Your Ears

A casual glance at the external human ear and that of the beagle or German shepherd reveals obvious differences. Although people's ears come in many shapes and sizes, the differences between Rocky Marciano's cauliflowers and Meryl Streep's dainty ones are far less dramatic than those between a Doberman's and a springer spaniel's.

The erect pinnae (ear flaps) of shepherds and Chihuahuas, the semidroop of shelties and borzois, and the floppy flaps of hounds all serve the same purpose as ours: they help channel sound into the ear canal. However, whereas we can, with a little imagination, picture the human pinna acting like a funnel for directing sound waves, it's hard to imagine that limp hound or poodle earflap doing the same. Because wild dogs, wolves, coyotes, and foxes all have erect ears, I suspect this is the contour that best enhanced sound collection, whereas the floppier flapped breeds belong to categories that are more likely dependent on some other sense. For example, I can understand why a protective earflap would be of value to scent hounds as they charge through the underbrush, nose to the ground and oblivious of thorns, seeds, or other matter that could damage the ear canal. Any decrease in hearing caused by the flap would easily be compensated for by the dog's increased sense of smell, and the flaps increased protective value to the ear.

Furthermore, the human and canine ear canals themselves differ dramatically. Although our ear canals provide a fairly straight shot to the eardrum which separates the canal from the inner ear, the dog's canal angles downward first.

This angled canal helps explain why some dogs have so many ear problems. An unknowledgeable owner armed with a Q-tip can force debris into that lateral canal where it's very hard to get out. In addition, some breeds such as poodles, Lhasa apsos, and Old English sheepdogs also have a great deal of hair at the canal opening, which can be problematic.

Although all that floppiness and hairiness may decrease the hearing of domestic dogs compared to that of their wild colleagues, even the most highly bred dog can hear much more than any human. A dog can hear within an estimated range of 20 to 50,000 cycles per second (cps) compared to a child's 30 to 20,000 cps range and a senior citizen's 50 to 8,000 cps. Over 95 percent of all dogs respond to a sound of 38,000 cycles per second, a sound that lies far beyond human perception. But frequency alone doesn't determine how much an individual can hear. Intensity makes a difference, too. As a general rule, a dog's ears are four and a half times more sensitive than our own. Think about that. Not only do our dogs hear many sounds we can't hear, they hear them for a longer duration than we do; a sound we lose track of 20 feet away can still attract the attention of a dog 80 feet away. Insensitive to this fact, most owners yell as loudly at a dog as they do at a child when they want it to stop misbehaving. Such screaming teaches a dog to behave about as effectively as teaching a three-year-old to count by screaming the numbers as loudly as possible in his ear. Not only wouldn't he learn what you wanted him to, he'd also become afraid of you.

The Nose Knows

What does relative size tell us about the importance of a sensory organ? Despite similarities in purpose, dog and people noses look different. Because the nose (and its countless paper-thin bony plates, specialized cells, nerves, and blood vessels) extends from its tip to the surface of the face, we can easily see that dog anatomy allows a lot more space for this sense than does the human facial structure—in fact, as much as 10 to 26 times more space, depending on the breed.

The dog's relatively poor vision leads it to depend on its keen sense of smell to hone in on specific objects and individuals. In the wild, a predator gains a clear advantage if it can identify its prey by scent before it embarks on an exhausting hunt. Have you ever chased a familiar-looking, tall, dark-haired man in a gray trench coat through rush hour traffic only to discover it's not Uncle Freddie? What a waste of time and energy! When a wild dog is chasing its dinner and there are only so many good hours of hunting in a day, it can't afford to waste time stalking or chasing inedible or otherwise undesirable prey.

Over the years people have bred dogs for certain looks without paying much attention to anatomy or even function. Such breeding has resulted in increased respiratory problems for the squashed-nosed brachycephalic breeds such as the boxer, pug, bulldog and Pekinese. These dogs have the same number of blood vessels, nerves, bony plates, and soft tissue in their olfactory (smelling) apparatus as longer-nosed breeds, but much less space to fit it all in. Even their nostrils are often abnormally small or deformed, limiting the amount of airborne scents that can stimulate their systems. Not only does all this cramming reduce the overall efficiency of the system, it inhibits the normal mechanisms for fighting off infection. Like people with colds, dogs with respiratory problems tend to lose some of their sense of smell.

You might expect that people bred the most needle-nosed (dolichocephalic) breeds such as collies, borzois, and dachshunds to perform functions highly dependent on a sense of smell, but that's not the case. These dogs were originally used for herding, hunting by sight, or digging prey out of burrows and dens. Interestingly enough, the true scent hounds such as beagles, redbones, and Plott hounds tend to have the more moderate (mesocephalic) noses.

Just as the dog's highly developed sense of smell compensates for its relatively poor detail vision, our much more specific vision compensates for our relatively poor sense of smell. These differences are bound to affect the way dogs and people create and respond to scent "pictures." In general, people tend to classify odors as good or bad based on their experience. For the Manhattan accountant raised on a farm in Wisconsin, the smell of manure at a Greenwich horse show triggers pleasant memories, whereas his city-bred wife may find the same odor repulsive.

Although dogs also respond to odors based on experience, they're born with a greater sensitivity to scents. More than 10 percent of the dog's brain is devoted to processing scent data compared with less than 1 percent of the human brain. Suppose our New York accountant and his wife take their eight-week-old pup for a walk. They barely get out the door before the pup begins to stop and sniff *everything*—sticks, stones, old bones, garbage, dirty sneakers, hydrants, and trees, places where it and other dogs have urinated and defecated. With its nose, the pup recreates a mental picture as detailed as the clearest photograph. It's able to differentiate not only various species of animals, but also different individuals from the same species. Urine odors on fenceposts or fire hydrants may convey important messages such as "Keep off. This is my territory!" As the pup matures, it learns to recognize that a specific odor change in its neighborhood means that the female down the street is coming into heat. Unfortunately, it won't recognize this dog as a buff cocker spaniel of championship breeding whose owners don't want it bred. On the other hand, the pup, unlike the female's owners, could easily identify her in a whole roomful of championship buff cockers.

What are the pup's owners doing while their dog strains its leash? They're shouting, "C'mon Bozo, let's go. It's getting dark and pretty soon we won't be able to see a thing!" Talk about the blind leading the deaf.

A Matter of Taste

Taste, like smell, can be highly subjective. Anatomically, both the human and canine senses of taste are located in the tongue. Unlike the eyes or ears, which function primarily as sense organs, however, the tongue does a lot of other jobs, too. Unlike people, dogs use their tongues to scoop up liquids and groom themselves, offspring, and friends. Not only does the tongue serve as a washcloth, brush, and comb, it replaces swabs and gauze as a means of cleansing wounds. Bitches use their tongues to stimulate nursing pups to urinate and defecate. And as if that weren't enough, the canine tongue also helps regulate body temperature via the panting mechanism.

Humans have evolved sophisticated and complex tastes for everything from fine wines to imported truffles, but can we expect our pets to appreciate these same tastes? Does a wild dog's taste need to distinguish anything more than the difference between safe and harmful substances? Does it seem reasonable that predators (which wild dogs surely are) can afford the luxury of passing up a meal because it's too salty or sweet? Understandably, when that wild dog evolves into a domestic one whose owner assigns all kinds of emotional overtones to what the dog eats, it finds itself in a rather bewildering predicament.

Humans projecting their own tastes on their dogs cause a host of problems. For example, the owner who loves broiled steak, french fries, or pizza too often assumes his or her dog will too. Unfortunately, such people-food doesn't suit the canine digestive system, nor does it fulfill the dog's nutritional needs. Sure, a dog will beg for table scraps and even seem to develop a fondness for Brie and crackers or beer, but it does so much less for the taste than for the interaction with its owner that invariably accompanies such feeding rituals.

On the other hand, owners often recoil in disgust when their dogs munch happily on bird droppings and dead mice, or lap contentedly around their own or another animal's anus and genitalia when, in fact, such behavior is perfectly normal and acceptable to dogs. The point to keep in mind is: are you projecting a people-meaning onto your dog's behavior? If so, you may misinterpret what your pet is trying to communicate via its sense of taste and discover the message it receives from you isn't what you intended at all.

Touch Me, Feel Me

Stroking and fondling, the warmth generated by physical contact, lie at the center of most loving human relationships. As we have seen with other senses, however, the canine and human responses to touch are both similar and different. In the case of touch, the differences don't derive as much from anatomical or physiological differences as from differences in interpretation. For children, touch can be either good or bad. Touching a parent's carelessly placed lighted cigarette causes pain, as does a swat on the rear end; from the child's point of view both sensations are bad. On the other hand, most of us assume children crave contact with adults and enjoy tickling, hugging, and cuddling.

However, assuming all animals instinctively like to be touched can cause communication breakdowns. For dogs, being touched is instinctively frightening and triggers a defensive reaction. In other words, dogs naturally respond to touch in one of three ways: they freeze, fight, or flee.

"But," you may be wondering, "I thought dogs were social [pack] animals?" They are, but keep in mind that many canine behaviors that worked in the wild may become negative behavioral tendencies in the household pet. Consider a litter of newborn pups. Up to the age of 2½ to 4 weeks of age, pups crawl all over each other with no defense reaction; but after this period, physical contact with one another results in defensive behavior. Why such a drastic behavioral change? For one thing, newborn pups have so little ability to regulate their body temperature that chilling almost always results in death; therefore, piling on top of one another helps guarantee survival. Once the pups fully develop the temperature-regulating mechanism by week 4, however, the laws of natural selection take over, and the pups vie for their positions within the litter and then within the pack. To survive in the wild, they must quickly establish dominant and submissive patterns of behavior. Weaker individuals must be eliminated or at least be kept from reproducing. Therefore, how the pups respond to the touch of others (whether they freeze, fight, or flee) determines both whether or not they survive, and their position within the pack. Researchers in animal behavior have discovered that the most dominant pups in a litter have the hardest time getting other pups to play with them because their aggressive advances elicit freeze, fight, or flee responses.

So how do domestic dogs learn *not* to react defensively when touched? They must be taught. Generally it happens automatically, if haphazardly. If the pups are born in a split-level condominium in Madison, Wisconsin, owners, kids, neighbors, and relatives usually begin handling them as soon as their eyes open. Professional breeders, on the other hand, often handle pups in specific ways for specific time periods daily to suppress the instinctive defense response. Still, many pups and dogs don't have this experience. We've all seen those shy dogs that huddle in the back of the cage or under the couch— you know, the ones we're so sure will melt into our arms in total contentment as soon as we pick them up. Beware: dogs or pups exhibiting such behavior are generally those who are the most submissive, those who lost ground when the pecking order was established. Like the aggressive pup which bounds right up and starts tugging on your shoe, this shy one may very well react defensively to your touch; instead of melting into your arms with a contented sigh, it may reward your efforts with a nasty bite.

Please notice I said this shy little pup is *as likely* to react defensively as the aggressive one. Remember, that dominant pup who runs right up to you earned that position by responding aggressively to the touch of its littermates. While the shy pup reacts defensively to touch because it took a beating when the pack order was being established, the aggressive one will be equally and perhaps more strongly defensive because it is much less tolerant of such behavior from others. Either way, you could get nipped.

No discussion of touch is complete without exploring the concept of pain. Unlike people, dogs don't automatically define pain as bad. For example, pups raised in isolation will repeatedly stick their noses into a lighted flame even after getting burned. However, in more natural surroundings they learn to respond to pain as a body signal, much as a driver learns that a red light means "Stop." Pain signals the dog to "Slow down," "Lay off the food for a few days," "Stay off that injured leg for a while." Pain is a natural lifesaver, not a threat. When a dog seems to react in pain to vaccinations, restraint, or minor injuries, it more than likely learned that response from people. If the pup utters a little yip of surprise (not pain) when it's vaccinated, and the owners communicate their anxiety over the response, they're unwittingly reinforcing the response in the pup, creating a dog who hates to go to the vet. Which comes first—the dog who hates to go to the vet or the owners who hate to take the dog to the vet?

Seeing Eye to Eye

Last but not least on our list of communicating senses is vision. We all know the importance of eye contact in human communication. On the surface, human and canine eyes seem to differ less than noses and ears. However, there are some major functional differences that strongly affect interspecies communication. If we measure the distance between the eyes of most dogs (except the brachycephalics), we see that dogs' eyes are further apart than humans'. As a result, dogs have about 20 percent less binocular (straight ahead) vision and 70 percent more peripheral (side) vision than we do. Both human and canine eyes contain a retina, consisting of specialized receptor cells called rods and cones. The rods distinguish motion, whereas the cones detect color and detail. Compared to the human retina, the dog's retina contains more rods than cones, making the dog much more adept at perceiving motion. People, on the other hand, can more easily perceive detail and color. Oddly enough, humans have lashes on both upper and lower lids, but seductive canines must be content with batting only an upper set of lashes.

If we remember that dogs enjoy greater peripheral and motion perception but less straight ahead and detail vision, we can easily understand how the two species see things differently. Because dogs respond more to movement (particularly to the sides) than we do, owners who discipline their pets by smacking them on the head or rump create interesting consequences for themselves and others. Because such dogs associate pain or discomfort with motion around their heads or rears, they react defensively to *any* motion toward those areas and, as we have seen, may display this defensiveness in an unacceptable way such as biting. If you wear glasses or have a beard, your dog's poor detail vision may lead it to make the same fearful response to your bespectacled neighbor or bearded brother-in-law. This phenomenon is called generalization: dogs that have bad or good experiences with one bearded man, toddler, uniformed mail carrier, bicycle, or UPS truck tend to respond defensively to similar people or objects. As we'll learn in later chapters, although generalization can create many headaches for the unknowledgeable owner, it can also provide a valuable tool for solving certain problems.

Body Language

All the senses play a role in what has come to be called "body language," the nonverbal cues and signals that can convey as much meaning as sights, sounds, smells, touches, and tastes. Just as people talk with their gestures, posture, and body movements, dogs talk with their carriage: the way it carries itself, those subtle ways it twitches its ears, tilts its head, or moves its tail, its different facial expressions. Have you ever noticed a dog that seems to be perpetually cowering or rolling over on its back at the slightest provocation? Such body language is common among wild dogs. In the wild this posture says, "I recognize your authority. I don't want to fight," a message that is vital to pack unity and survival. After all, in order to function at maximum efficiency, a group can follow only so many leaders, and the whole group benefits from recognizing leaders and followers. Obeying such body language enables dogs to avoid that common nonproductive human group situation in which everybody ends up shouting, "Who's in charge here?" Pity the poor owner who sees submissive body language in his dogs as the wrong message: "I'm a coward and I'm peeing to get even with you."

One of the more delightful forms of body language is smiling. Some dogs pull their upper lips back in a big grin in response to lavish praise. Its effect on people can be astonishing. The first time I experienced it, I jumped back thinking, "My God, this dog's baring her teeth; she's going to bite me!" Luckily, everything else in the dog's posture told me the animal was thinking no such thing. Such "smiling" may be another primitive sign of submission that's made it into certain domestic dogs. However, because all of the smiling dogs I have met are animals of exceptionally stable temperament, I don't associate this behavior with fear at all. I have never seen an animal displaying this trait give any indication it would bite; quite the contrary, they seem to smile only when they're happy and contented, just like we do.

The Many Splendored Thing

"If I speak in the tongues of men and of angels but have not love, I am a noisy gong or a clanging cymbal." These words reminded early Christians that communication involves much more than the mere exchange of words and ideas. There are probably as many definitions and descriptions of love as there are people on this earth. The one I think offers the most value for dog owners comes from a social worker I know who counsels people with seemingly insurmountable problems:

"Love's the exception and the rule. It's the safety valve. If strong love exists, you can make lots of mistakes and things still work out all right. It may take more or less time to solve problems, but love guarantees they *will* be solved."

It's impossible to speak of the role love plays in communication without simultaneously recognizing the inextricable bond that exists between love and confidence. Like love, confidence springs from a secure belief that we understand what we're doing and why, and that it's the right thing for us and our pets. By the same token, dogs who believe that the behavior desired by their owners is natural and/or acceptable, accomplish that behavior happily.

Teaching and learning arising from love, patience, and confidence can create sensational communication. Did one of your teachers or relatives ever show how much he or she cared by patiently teaching you some small skill despite your clumsiness and mistakes, and share your joy at your successes? Bring that same attitude to training your dog. You get out what you put in.

It's surprising how many people think of pups (especially purebred or expensive ones) as canine seedlings one merely feeds and waters and periodically fertilizes (i.e., trains a bit), which automatically grow into well-behaved adults. We only obtain well-mannered adults after a major investment of time and thought: no deposit, no return.

Not training a pup produces four negative results:

• a destructive dog, a nuisance, and possibly a threat to others
• an unconfident dog
• an unconfident and guilt-ridden owner
• a poor canine/human relationship

Would any dog owner deliberately submit him or herself or a dog to any of these consequences? Not deliberately perhaps, yet we see evidence of the inadvertent results every day. Although all dog owners expect to do some training, if they view teaching and learning as a chore rather than a joy, they don't invest the necessary time and thoughtfulness in any training program. Some lose interest after housebreaking, some never even get that far. Others don't worry about training until the dog destroys a favorite rug or bites a child. Training a dog in response to misbehavior in lieu of educating it properly in the first place replaces love and confidence with fear and guilt—exactly the wrong state of mind for effective communication.

We know we're more intelligent than our dogs, so why do we have so much trouble teaching them? Why do all our good intentions so often go up in smoke? Most of us falter at the outset because we never really *decide* to train the dog as a means of expressing love. Sound simple? Unfortunately, we often stumble over this obvious decision because we suspect a dog's education requires a major commitment of time and energy and indicates a deficit in both the dog and ourselves. So we casually say, "Someone should teach this dog not to jump up" or "I ought to teach Plasmatic not to pee on the rug." Such halfhearted commitments can't possibly lead to lasting results. If we decide we *want* a trained dog, we must commit ourselves to that decision.

The Four Basic Options

At some point in the process of making a decision about how to deal with your dog, you must consider what I call the Four Basic Options:

- Am I willing to accept the present situation (the dog's behavior or my relationship with it) and my feelings about it?
- Am I willing to change my feelings and accept what I now consider unacceptable?
- Am I willing to change my own and/or my dog's

behavior to align it with my definition of acceptable?
* Do I want to get rid of the dog?

These are four of the most important questions to consider when evaluating your relationship with your dog, and we'll be referring to them time and time again. Choosing the option you think is the best one for you and your dog opens the first channel of communication; if you don't see any problem in your relationship with your dog, regardless what anyone else says about it, you're not going to commit yourself to making any changes, and if you don't really want the dog, you'll never make a commitment to change, either. Successful training invariably involves *consistent* love and confidence from which change for both dog and owner can arise. If the love and confidence aren't there from the beginning, the dog may become fully *disciplined*, but never a fully communicating canine companion.

In the next chapter, we'll lay the groundwork for determining the difference between the things we can change and the things we can't. Then we'll see how to change the ones we can and accept the others. Echoing this philosophy, the Beatles put it another way: all you need is love.

The Communication-Behavior Link

Bob and Lorena Goodman love playing tug of war with Ralphie, their two-year-old terrier mix. As a pup Ralphie was reluctant to play, so the Goodmans began dragging an old towel slowly across the floor, then praising and petting the dog when he pounced on it.

"Good boy, Ralphie," crowed Bob.

"Isn't Ralph the greatest dog?" Lorena gushed to their guests. "Watch this trick." Everyone laughed when the dog shook the towel so hard it sent Lorena sprawling on the rug.

Then one morning Ralphie demolished Lorena's favorite sweater while his mistress was still asleep and Bob was in the shower. When Bob emerged from the bathroom and saw the shredded cashmere in Ralphie's mouth, he began swatting the dog with his wet towel. Ralphie grabbed the towel and yanked on it, thinking his master wanted to play their favorite game.

"Bad dog, Ralph! Stop it! Bad, bad!"

All the commotion woke Lorena, who yelled at Bob to stop hitting the dog; but when she saw her ruined sweater, she switched her attention to Ralphie.

"Bad, bad boy. How could you do this to me?" Snatching the sweater, she threw it at the terrified Ralphie who by this time was scurrying under the bed.

"I don't know," said Bob sadly, "Ralph's usually a good dog, but sometimes he seems dumber than a stump."

If you're like most dog owners, you've probably experienced similar episodes with your pet. In fact, such events occur so frequently that many people accept them as a normal, if uncomfortable, part of dog ownership. Some days our dogs seem so intelligent; other days, they act like complete idiots. And all it takes is a succession of dumb-dog days, even over a period of years, to lead us to think there's something wrong with us, the dog, or both. When such doubt arises, guilt invariably follows on its heels, leading us to wonder whether owning a dog is worth the hassle.

Let's take a closer look at the Goodmans' little skirmish with Ralphie to understand how communication broke down.

A Potpourri of Praise and Punishment

When they brought their puppy home, Bob and Lorena used the standard old-fashioned training methods: yelling and swatting. They didn't abuse Ralphie, but they did use a rolled-up newspaper to swat him on the rump when he misbehaved; they also used the paper to smack the counter or tabletop to distract him from bad behavior. In both cases the Goodmans sternly admonished the dog with phrases such as "No, Ralphie!," "Ralph, stop that!," and "Bad dog!" On the other hand, whenever his owners wanted to show Ralphie they were pleased, Lorena gently stroked the terrier's head or Bob engaged him in a rough and tumble romp on the floor. Ralphie's good behavior also earned him treats and enthusiastic compliments such as "Atta boy!," "Way to go, Ralph!," and "What a good dog!" Like most puppies, Ralphie was such a lovable bundle of fur that Bob, Lorena, and their friends spent a great deal of time playing with him and laughing at his antics. In fact, Ralphie's name came up in almost every conversation. "Isn't Ralphie the cutest thing?" "Guess what Ralphie did this morning!"

Doesn't this seem like perfectly natural owner behavior? It may be, but let's examine it more closely to see how natural it is for Ralphie. Because a dog's hearing is more than four times more sensitive than ours, does loudness affect Ralphie the same way it does us? Hardly. And remember the dog's normal tactile response? Touch elicits an instinctively defensive response, telling Ralphie to freeze, fight, or flee from the source. It does *not* tell him "Don't chew, bark, or scratch." To be sure, a smart pup can eventually *learn* to make these associations, but they're not part of its natural instincts. Similarly, when Lorena and Bob stroke or play with Ralphie, the dog must first subordinate his natural defenses before accepting such actions as positive gestures.

What happens if the Goodmans use loud sounds and touch to communicate *both* pleasure and displeasure to their dog? Because both cues naturally elicit defensive responses, Ralphie must learn to ignore these before he can figure out what response his owners do want. That's like hearing the words "Look out!" used to mean "Hi, how are you?" You must first acknowledge there is no danger before you can recognize the completely different meaning these words are meant to convey.

If we examine the phrases Bob and Lorena use to praise and discipline Ralphie as well as their tendency to speak about the dog between themselves and among friends, we discover another common practice that interferes with effective owner-dog communication. Although we often expect quite specific responses from our dogs, we simultaneously offer them the most generalized cues. For example, the Goodmans expect Ralphie to respond whether they call him Ralphie, Ralph, dog, boy, or idiot. In other words, they expect him to recognize that all these names refer to him. When they issue the commands "No!" "Stop that!" or "Move!" they also expect the dog to understand immediately what they're talking about. To further complicate matters, they expect him to understand the difference between these words as well as his various names, whether they're addressed to him, each other, or some third party.

Can we owners rightfully assume our dogs can make such subtle distinctions? Remember, we're dealing with a species whose *hearing*, not its *intelligence*, may be far superior to ours. Just because Ralphie can hear his owners doesn't mean he understands them. It's going to take him a while to figure out that Ralphie, Ralph, dog, boy, and idiot all refer to him, and he'll gradually do that by learning to respond to his owners' tone or inflections as much as what they say. What if the Goodmans embellish their general conversation with similar words, tones, and inflections? At first Ralphie perks up his ears, but when he realizes the speaker's attention lies elsewhere, he soon learns to ignore the word, the tone and inflection, and eventually even the owners.

Orienting and Listening: Getting Back on the Same Track

We can avoid these problems by understanding and utilizing the concepts of orienting and listening. How do we orient dogs? Because the canine world revolves around perceptions, we use its senses. For example, the Goodmans use sound when they orient Ralphie using his name. However, to do so they must be sure to use one and only one name or word to attract or orient the dog's attention. This means the Goodmans must decide whether they call Ralphie "Ralphie" because he looks like a Ralphie, or because they want to be known as people who own a dog named Ralphie. If the former is the case, then they should only use the word "Ralphie" when they want the dog's attention. On the other hand, if they prefer to refer to their dog as Ralphie in casual conversation between themselves and among friends, then they should call the dog "Hector," "Caruso," or some other name, or use some word such as "Shazam!" or "Hup!" to orient him with sound.

Although using the dog's name, a whistle, or some other sound is the most common form of orientation, other senses may also be used. Most owners feel they have a dog's attention if it's looking right at them; that's visual orientation and the cornerstone of the highly specialized communication occurring between deaf people and their hearing dogs. Expert tracking dogs like Trep who sniffed out $63 million worth of narcotics have been taught to orient to scent cues as have thousands of pudgy canines who loll between stove and refrigerator when meals are being prepared. Owners who train dogs with treats orient with taste as well as smell, whereas those who smack their dogs to "get their attention" orient using the sense of touch.

Although most owners automatically orient a dog one way or another, *choosing* to orient it *consistently* in a *specific* way provides a most valuable tool. Doing so communicates to the dog that a given sound, sight, scent, taste, or touch means "Pay attention." I like to think of orientation as the key unlocking the door between me and my dog. It doesn't guarantee that the dog receives the right message, but at least it clears the way for a message to be sent.

The other half of orientation involves paying attention to our dogs, learning about their needs and their peculiar messages and being willing to let them orient us at times. Some owners feel it's necessary that the dog perceives things exactly the way they do. When they say a certain word, they want the dog to respond a certain way. How many times have we shouted in frustration, "When I say sit, *I Mean SIT!*" To us, sit means the dog bends its rear legs and places its rump on the floor. When the dog doesn't do that, we automatically assume it's stupid, it's stubborn, it doesn't respect our authority, or that it wants to make us angry. Suppose "Sit" means something entirely different to the dog. What if the loud hissing noise elicits an instinctive *defense* response, so when the Goodmans shout at Ralphie, "I SAID SIT!," the pup receives the message: "They want to hurt me." What a far cry from the owner's interpretation, "Bend your rear legs and put your rump on the floor."

Consider another example. Poor hip conformation isn't

uncommon in large dogs, and if the condition is pronounced, a young animal may experience all the limitations and discomfort of an older animal with severe arthritis. In both cases, the normal sitting position may take some time to assume, and the dog may prefer to lie down instead. Owners who aren't willing to listen to their dogs automatically expect such animals to respond quickly to their "Sit!" command and are invariably frustrated.

To develop your listening skills, ask yourself two questions:

- What am I communicating to my dog?
- What is my dog communicating to me?

When the Goodmans ask themselves these questions regarding Ralphie's destructive chewing and their response to it, they answer the first: "We want him to know his chewing makes us mad." They want Ralphie to realize he's destroying something they value, creating extra work, costing them money, and making them unhappy. In other words, they want their dog to feel guilty. But can dogs feel human guilt? Even if they can, does guilt facilitate learning?

If they want to make Ralphie aware of their anger, they can communicate this by jumping up and down, screaming, or smacking him; but if they want to communicate "Stop the chewing because it bothers us," they can use a much more effective method. In the first case all they convey is emotion; in the second, the Goodmans convey a desire for a definite behavioral change. Always listen to yourself and what you're saying. If it's not clear to you, it's surely not going to be clear to your dog.

What is Ralphie communicating to the Goodmans? Is he being spiteful, stubborn, and stupid? Those are hu-

man emotions used by humans to describe human behavior, and we can make some big communication mistakes when we transfer those prejudices to our pets. Not
only do such concepts mean little or nothing to our dogs,
they block our understanding of normal canine perception and behavior necessary to solve many common problems. When your dog communicates, pay attention. Rather
than judging its response emotionally, try to imagine its
point of view.

Inconsistency: When Yesterday's Yes Becomes Today's No

Having initially established confusing communication
with Ralphie, the Goodmans fall prey to the dog owner's
greatest nemesis: inconsistency. Dog owners can achieve
good results with even the worst training methods as
long as they're consistent. For example, every neighborhood has a beautifully behaved dog whose owner bru-
tally snaps its choke collar the instant the dog makes the
slightest misstep. From the moment the dog entered the
household as a pup, the owner made it quite clear *all*
behavior would be dealt with immediately and in the
same way. By consistently receiving this punishment any
time its behavior ran counter to its owner's wishes, the
dog has learned to focus on the owner, even ignoring its
natural instincts. Although I strongly disapprove of the
use of pain in training, the existence of well-behaved
animals trained by such methods proves the point that
the key isn't the method; it's the consistent application
of that method.

When Bob and Lorena use five different names for
Ralphie, when they use the same phrase to mean dif-

ferent things, or when they reward a certain behavior today but condemn it and Ralphie tomorrow, their inconsistency inhibits any kind of meaningful communication. When Ralphie plays tug-of-war with an old towel, his owners praise him; but when he shreds a cashmere sweater, they swat him with another towel that looks just like his favorite plaything. Unfortunately, the Goodmans forget Ralphie's eyes respond primarily to motion, making one lump of cloth look pretty much like another. When Bob and Lorena praise Ralphie's tug-of-war play with the towel, the dog expects them to respond positively whenever those same conditions arise; in other words, Ralphie is intuitively or naturally consistent and expects similar behavior from others. The fact that Ralphie can't distinguish an old towel from a good one or even a sweater means that his criteria for the game are quite different from his owners'. As far as Ralphie is concerned, all it should take to please his owners is his tugging on a piece of material; he expects their consistent praise under these circumstances. When Bob and Lorena enthusiastically praise him one time (when it's an old towel) and punish him another (when it's a piece of clothing or a good towel), Ralphie becomes confused. To him, there's not enough difference in his behavior or the conditions surrounding it to warrant such radically different responses.

Now let's see how inconsistency can compound problems arising from differences between the human and animal senses of taste. Bob and Lorena regularly eat pizza while watching Monday night football, and during commercials Ralphie does tricks for slices of pepperoni. Sometimes he even gets the leftover pizza after the game. One Monday, Lorena prepares a gourmet pizza, but just as she places it on the coffee table in front of the television, the phone rings. "Good dog," she mutters distractedly to Ralphie as she rushes past him in the hall. By the time she finishes the call, Ralphie has dragged the pizza to the floor and whatever he hasn't eaten now sticks to the new braided rug. That pizza was the only food in the house, and the carpet cost the Goodmans over five hundred dollars. What would you do in Lorena's place? Before you answer, carefully consider both your normal methods of communicating with your dog and your dog's normal responses to those methods. What senses come into play in this situation?

In Bob and Lorena's case, the sense of taste plays a part in their communication with Ralphie. If he performs his tricks, they reward him with pizza, making pizza more than mere food to the dog. Food is that dry stuff sitting in his dish at all times, but pizza equals love. And didn't his mistress tell him he was a good dog when he was on his way into the living room? Well, Lorena went berserk when she saw the pizza-stained rug, grabbed poor Ralphie by the scruff of the neck, and rubbed his nose in the mess and smacked him, just as if he had broken house-training. Let's look at the different ways inconsistency compounds this problem:

- The Goodmans praised Ralphie for eating the food under one set of circumstances and punished him for eating that same food under different circumstances.
- Lorena disciplined the dog for eating the food after she gave the positive "Good dog" blessing to his activities.
- Lorena made the previously positive food negative by forcing Ralphie's face into it while smacking and yelling at him.

- The final and most confusing inconsistency of all is that the Goodmans expect the dog never to eat pizza from the table again. However, they also expect him to respond just as positively to the Monday night tidbits offered on *their* terms.

The best way to avoid inconsistency is to keep things simple. Always use the same words or objects to mean the same things under all circumstances. If you use pizza to communicate with your dog, then always have it mean the same thing. If you use food this way, then it should always be either a reward or a punishment. For example, during the preferred Monday night ritual Ralphie develops strong positive feelings about pizza because he receives a lot of love along with the pepperoni and cheese. Were Bob and Lorena to smack Ralphie every time they had pizza, the dog would soon learn to quake at his first whiff of pepperoni and cower submissively at the mere sight of the cheese.

So strong are the emotional associations we humans make with food and taste that their transference to our canine companions causes major problems. We'll discuss this phenomenon in detail in Chapter 7; for now, recognize that the simplest, most consistent way to avoid food-related problems is to feed the dog the same dog food in the same way every day.

Whenever I see people embroiled in unnerving problems with their dogs due to inconsistent use and interpretation of the senses, I recall Sigmund Freud's elaborate theory that dreams embody much sexual symbolism. As time went on, colleagues and reporters could find hidden meaning in any dream. Attempting to put things back into their proper perspective, Freud halted a conversation by saying, "Sometimes a cigar is just a cigar."

Dog owners can enhance and simplify their communication with their dogs by remembering that dogs respond best to sounds, sights, tastes, smells, and touches which have only one meaning. Such a simplified and consistent approach to communication can eliminate many common problems.

Normal versus Natural: Mixed Signals

In Chapter One we observed some common characteristics of the canine senses. We also learned how these natural senses evolved, how increased peripheral, motion-sensitive vision, acute hearing, and a defensive response to touch assisted animals who prey upon others and must keep from being preyed upon themselves. In the wild, beneficial characteristics persisted and detrimental ones diminished or disappeared altogether. Although the relationship between the senses and behavioral patterns is complex, natural selection tends to change whatever doesn't work and maintain whatever does. People evolved one way, dogs another. Unfortunately, people sometimes forget the differences and define what is normal for the dog in human terms.

No matter how sensitive and knowledgeable dog owners become, they often find it very difficult not to determine what's normal for the dog in terms of their own beliefs. If Bob Goodman responds to his mother's "Robert," his co-workers' "Bob," and his wife's "Rob," why shouldn't Ralphie be able to respond to his various names? If we find stool and urine repulsive, why should it appeal to our dogs? If we can only hear a certain relatively narrow range of sounds, why shouldn't we expect our dogs to ignore all others? If we enjoy steak and french fries, why shouldn't the dog? The answers to such questions lead many owners to view *normal* training as aligning their dogs' perceptual world with their own. That's sort of like putting your teenage brother's souped-up '69 Chevy on the Grand Prix circuit. The Chevy may have meaning in your brother's world, but the only message it conveys in the Grand Prix is that it doesn't belong; regardless of what we do to the Chevy, it can never be a formula race car. Similarly, regardless of our human expectations for our dogs, our dogs will never be human. If we expect them to be like us, we'll always be disappointed. If we let them be dogs and create an environment where they can manifest their canine nature to best complement our human qualities, we'll invariably enjoy the results.

Setting the Standards for Basic Communication

Knowledge and sensitivity provide the keys to opening and maintaining effective channels of interspecies communication:

- Knowledge of our dogs' senses and how they differ from our own.
- Sensitivity to any inconsistencies between our expectations and our dogs' abilities to respond.
- Knowledge of normal canine versus human behavior.

Armed with these, you can effectively evaluate your existing relationship with your dog: not the way it was before you moved into the condominium, not the way you dream it could be, but the way it is right now. Simply stand back and take a cold, hard look at the current state of things between you and your pet. Like the Goodmans, you'll find that communication lies at the core of most of your problems.

In the following chapters, we'll discover that even though communication is at the root of many problems, it's also the key to solving them. This may sound a lot more mundane than using a three hundred dollars shock collar or a canine macrobiotic diet, but it works. Once you're able to communicate with your dog, you have a workable basis for adjusting your relationship.

How can you tell if your present relationship is mutually acceptable? That's simple: Is it working? Are you happy with your relationship with your dog? Once the Goodmans learn to isolate the different ways they and Ralphie communicate, they can begin to identify things they want to change, things they want to keep the way they are, and those they probably can't change even if they want to. Whatever they decide to change, they'll find that more effective communication will achieve healthy, permanent results.

To Accept or Not To Accept

The Feldsteins' Yorkshire terrier Disraeli sleeps on his owners' bed when they're gone. "George absolutely hates it," says his wife, Inez. "Every time we come home, George sneaks into the house and tries to catch the dog. After five years of this, it's become a game."

Privately George adds, "When the little bugger started this, I think I would have killed him if I found him on my bed. Now, even though it still irks the hell out of me, I'd be a little disappointed if I actually caught him."

So even though the Feldsteins define Disraeli's presence on the bed as a problem and George acknowledges he doesn't like it, both the behavior and their feelings about it have become an acceptable part of their lives.

Compare this to Pete d'Alesandro's response to his exuberant black lab, Rugby. At first, every time Rugby took off to visit the dog next door, Pete threw a fit. He was embarrassed by his dog's behavior and apologetic to his neighbors. He was disappointed by his inability to train the dog, angry with Rugby for taking off, and felt guilty about punishing the dog to relieve his own frustrations. When Pete's neighbors assured him their female was spayed and that Rugby was a welcome companion for their dog, Pete finally grew to accept Rugby's behavior as normal and beneficial.

No matter how great or small the problem, we must invariably confront the Four Basic Options discussed in Chapter 1:

- Am I willing to accept the present situation (the dog's behavior or my relationship with it) and my feelings about it?
- Am I willing to change my feelings and accept what I now consider unacceptable?
- Am I willing to change my own and/or my dog's behavior to align it with my definition of acceptable?
- Do I want to get rid of the dog?

The majority of training methods speak to owners like the Friehoffers who choose the third option and want to change their Chin-Chin, Mee Tu's, chewing behavior. Mee Tu has already destroyed two handmade afghans and is gnawing her way through a third. Aside from this, the entire Friehoffer family finds no fault with the dog.

No one wants to give her up, yet they'll never accept the destruction of family heirlooms either. In cases such as this, the owners choose to train Mee Tu not to chew, to align her behavior with their own wishes.

Over the years I've encountered enough dog/owner relationships to know that sometimes the fourth choice—getting rid of the dog—can be the best for all concerned. When Alonzo, the keeshond, becomes so blind, deaf, and arthritic that even the slightest touch or movement causes him to recoil in terror, the *quality* has disappeared from the shared communication between dog and humans. Instead of enriching Alonzo's life, his few remaining senses send and receive one message: "Look out! Don't touch me there. I'm afraid." Not a pleasant world to be living in.

Like it or not, divorce can make sense. Does divorce mean the parties don't believe in marriage? To the contrary; if one holds high ideals for marriage, but the marriage brings suffering, divorce can be a strong affirmation of one's ideals. People receive dogs as gifts every day, and many of these people never would have chosen these dogs. Such owners may feel compelled to make the best of the situation, but dishonestly preserving an incompatible relationship seldom benefits either party. Because the commitment to the pet isn't present, there's no desire to develop a lasting relationship, or any form of meaningful communication. Owners who tolerate a relationship out of some false sense of guilt or obligation aren't doing themselves or their dogs any favors. Dogs, like people, possess that keen ultrasense: love. If the relationship and the communication isn't sincere, everyone knows it.

Reinhold Niebuhr's famous prayer offers us all some good advice: "Lord, grant me the serenity to accept the things I cannot change, the courage to change the things I can, and the wisdom to know the difference." The first step to accepting or changing any part of our relationships with our dogs involves making a conscious choice to do so. Without the resolve and commitment that come from choice, you'll never be able to consistently accept certain behaviors or consistently train yourself or your dog to change them.

Now that we understand how communication affects behavior, let's see how the six-step problem-solving method can work for you.

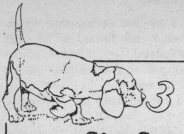

Six Steps to Solving Any Problem with Your Dog

Tim and Sherry Bardwell bought their golden retriever, Christi, when she was a fuzzy ball of fur, and they can't imagine a more adorable or lovable pet. Unfortunately, whenever the Bardwells or any other person or dog enters their apartment, Christi immediately squats and dribbles urine. Tim and Sherry wouldn't mind so much if their front door didn't open directly into the living room, smack in the middle of which sits a cherished Oriental rug, a wedding present from Tim's parents. Christi has received countless scoldings and spankings for this behavior and, after four months of Christi's daily staining and Sherry's spot cleaning, the rug looks like a reject from a yard sale. Tim imagines his mother's horrified reaction should his parents unexpectedly pop in for a visit.

"I love Christi," sighs Tim. "But she's getting worse. Now she even pees when I walk toward her. I can't understand why she's so spiteful."

"Maybe you should stop yelling at her and hitting her when she's bad," replies his wife.

"Ah, she does it when you talk baby talk to her too, Sherry!"

"I know. But she's not spiteful. She's just stupid. Maybe we should send her to obedience school."

"Or to the pound."

"Never!" snaps Sherry, clutching the struggling pup to her breast. "Nobody's going to hurt my widdle snookims."

The Bardwells have a problem. In this chapter we're going to help Tim and Sherry study and solve it step by step, and by the time we're done, we'll have a general procedure that works for all sorts of problems, not only the ones in this book, but all the unusual ones you may experience with your pet. Although a stepwise procedure may seem overly formal, such a strategy can help us avoid the temptation to instantaneously jump from problem to solution.

In our example, the Bardwells have adopted a time-honored procedure for solving their problem: when Christi dribbles urine, Tim yells and swats her behind. Christi squats lower and dribbles more, infuriating Tim into more yelling and hitting. This makes Sherry feel so guilty, she cuddles the dog and coos to her as soon as the commotion dies down, even though this also makes the dog urinate. Because the behavior still persists after four months, it's safe to say the old-fashioned approach has failed. Let's see if we can help the Bardwells find a better method before this one puts Christi behind bars.

Step One: Recognize the Existing Behavior as Normal

Remember the importance of determining what's normal for you and your dog? That's the first and most difficult step toward the solution of any problem. Whether the Bardwells like it or not, it's *normal* for Christi to urinate on the rug when people or animals enter the house, when Tim yells at or hits her, or when Sherry babies her. Notice how we avoid adding value judgments such as good, bad, spiteful, or stupid to our definition of the behaviors of the humans or canine involved. I can't overemphasize this point. Even with all my experience with the full spectrum of dog/owner problems, I still have to remind myself to eliminate such judgments before I evaluate even the most repulsive behavior.

"It's *not* normal for dogs to pee in the house!" storms Tim, who certainly doesn't want to be known as the owner of a dog who does. But Tim is projecting his own values on his dog, something every owner finds hard to avoid. Nonetheless, the Bardwells can't begin to solve their problem until they stop projecting those human beliefs and open themselves to Christi's canine way of seeing things.

Owners who define the dog's behavior, their response to it, or both as bad or abnormal automatically define themselves and their dogs as bad or abnormal, thereby getting the problem solving off to a negative start. Not surprisingly, those who learn to define problem behavior as normal gain a tremendous psychological advantage. Whatever the problem, a positive approach achieves quicker and more lasting results. That sounds reasonable, but it's not as easy as it sounds. Even if we owners can free ourselves from value judgments regarding our dogs' behavior, we usually find it a lot more difficult to free ourselves from the judgments of others. If ninety-nine out of a hundred people who live in the Bardwells' apartment complex define house soiling as abnormal, then Tim and Sherry will feel a lot of pressure to agree with them. I've encountered hundreds of owners who worked out satisfactory, if unconventional, relationships with their dogs only to suffer from the almost universal disapproval of other people. One such owner told me: "I love to sleep with my spaniel, but my girl friend says that's so disgusting, *she* won't sleep with me anymore." Talk about pressure!

Let's assume Tim and Sherry accomplish step one. They immediately eliminate much of the time-consuming and unproductive emotion that hinders problem solving. Unencumbered by this emotion, they're free to concentrate all their efforts on objectively defining the problem and finding the best solution as quickly as possible.

Step Two: Define the Problem

Compared to step one, defining the problem is a snap, but it can still be tricky because sometimes the main problem gets caught up in other issues. To determine whether your definition of the problem tells the whole story, keep asking "Why?" and "When?" For example, Tim and Sherry initially define the problem as Christi's spitefulness and stupidity. But is it? Let's play detective, repeatedly asking the Bardwells *why* they think Christi is spiteful and stupid:

"Because she keeps peeing in the house," they respond.

"Why?"

"Because she's spiteful and stupid."

"Why?"

"Because Tim hits her?"

"Because Sherry babies her?"

"Why?"

"Because we scare her or make her nervous?"

Although we haven't precisely defined the problem, we have moved from an insoluble one (spitefulness and stupidity) to a soluble one ("nervous" urination). Remember our Four Basic Options? Owners who define their dogs' problems as spitefulness, stupidity, or meanness leave themselves no alternatives beyond resigning themselves to flaws or getting rid of their dogs.

Once we've defined the problem as soluble, we can ask a series of "When?" questions.

"Hmmm," says Tim, "What else makes Christi pee in the house?"

"*When* does she do it?"

"When people come in the front door."

"When else?"

"When she sees other dogs."

Now we're cooking. Tim and Sherry are pinpointing the conditions that cause the behavior. Let's ask some more "Why?" questions:

"Why does she dribble on these occasions?"

Tim thinks about that for a while. "I dunno. What do they all have in common?"

"I wonder," says Sherry. "When people visit, she's

really happy if she recognizes them and scared silly if she doesn't. The same with other dogs. And of course, she's scared stiff when you yell at her, but she seems so happy when I'm cooing at her."

"That's it!" shouts Tim. "She dribbles when she's excited *or* scared. When she experiences strong feelings of any kind!"

Having gained this insight, the Bardwells can now evaluate the major parts of Christi's problem behavior. Methodical Tim decides to list what he and Sherry have discovered:

Problem	When the Problem Occurs/ Occurred	Possible Explanation(s)
Christie pees in the house.	When people or dogs visit.	She's frightened or excited.
	When Tim yells at her.	She's frightened.
	When Tim hits her.	She's frightened.
	When Sherry babies her.	She's excited.
Christie is ruining the rug.	Same as for first problem.	Same as for first problem.

With the problem clearly defined, Tim and Sherry can now consider some possible solutions.

Step Three: List All Possible Solutions

Before considering various solutions, Tim and Sherry ponder the Four Basic Options:

"We can never put up with that smell, or a dog that pees in the house," say the Bardwells, "but we really love Christi and don't want to get rid of her." That leaves them with the third alternative: changing canine and/or human behavior.

Like step two, we can pose a target question to help us zero in on the most effective solutions: *How* can we change our own or our dog's behavior? Completing yet another list helps us examine each component of the problem separately. For instance, how can the Bardwells keep visitors from scaring or exciting Christi? How can Tim and Sherry behave differently toward Christi? When listing alternative solutions, put down every one that comes to mind, even if it seems silly, because including all alternatives eventually helps you determine the most effective one. Here's the Bardwells' list.

Problem	*Possible Solution(s)*
When people excite or scare Christi, she pees.	—Don't have visitors.
	—Put Christi outdoors when people arrive.
	—Have those who scare Christi make friends with her.
	—Have those who delight her discourage her advances.
	—Have all visitors ignore her.

When other dogs excite or scare her, Christi pees.	—Don't allow dogs to visit.
	—Put Christi outside when dogs visit.
	—Allow only nonthreatening or easygoing dogs to visit.
	—Let the dogs work it out outside.
Tim's yelling scares Christi into dribbling.	—Stop yelling.
Tim's hitting prompts peeing.	—Stop hitting.
Sherry's baby talk excites Christi into dribbling.	—Stop baby talk.
Christi's peeing is ruining the rug.	—Cover the rug.
	—Keep Christi out of the living room.
	—Thoroughly clean the rug.
	—Put the rug away.

Notice how Tim and Sherry don't have much choice when they address the third, fourth, and fifth problems. Most owners who realize the dog's behavior results from differences in perception rather than stupidity or spitefulness quite willingly consider stopping their own contributing behavior. Although Tim doesn't completely understand why his yelling makes Christi urinate, as soon as he recognizes that it does, he's eager to change his behavior to help solve the problem. Similarly, Sherry doesn't mind altering her manner of talking to the dog if that will help remedy the situation. At this point the Bardwells have based their decision to change their behavior on observation rather than information; they know Christi doesn't dribble urine if they don't excite or frighten her. Removing the stimulus, for whatever reason, should automatically reduce the response. Already owners and dog have opened fresh lines of communication.

Step Four: Collect Information

When Tim and Sherry study their list of problems and alternative solutions, they conclude that changing their own behavior shortens the list to three major problem areas: (1) Christi's reaction to visitors; (2) her reaction to other dogs; and (3) the rug. Let's examine the possible solutions to each component.

"We can't break off our friendships," insists Tim.

"And we can't put her outdoors every time the doorbell rings," adds Sherry. "Even if we could, that's cruel."

Thus the Bardwells eliminate all but three of their possible solutions for further study:

- Have those who scare Christi make friends with her.
- Have those who delight her discourage her advances.
- Have all visitors ignore her.

After defining the problem and isolating possible solutions, the owners begin collecting information that will highlight the reasons why one or another solution might work best. Owners setting up a research program have a lot of resources at their command. Most libraries offer a wide selection of books on animal behavior and dog training which can be very helpful. Veterinarians, breeders, and other dog owners can also provide information. Be sure to collect enough data to make you feel comfortable with your ultimate solution. The more faith you have in any solution, the more easily you can *consistently* implement it.

"What's wrong with trial and error?" asks Tim. Although trial-and-error methods might eventually produce results, they can have a devastating effect on the dog. Never forget the importance of consistency. Suppose the Bardwells invite some friends over, instructing those who were formerly quite friendly to Christi to discourage her advances, while telling those who frightened the dog to descend on her with lavish displays of love. Such sudden and conflicting changes in human behavior could totally unnerve the dog and create a new problem—a dog who hides under the bed and urinates every time the doorbell rings.

Thorough research helps you determine what message your dog is trying to communicate through the behavior as well as what you're communicating to the dog through your response. Sherry decides to call the kennel where they bought Christi to see if the breeder can shed some light on the problem.

"All puppies do that," says the breeder after Sherry describes Christi's problem. "Don't worry; she'll outgrow it."

Sherry persists. "But why do they do it?"

"When they're babies they only urinate when their mother licks their rear ends. That stimulates the pups to release urine and stool, which the mother laps up when she cleans them. If she doesn't do this, the pups don't relieve themselves and may even become ill because of waste product buildup."

"She laps it up? Oh yuck, why doesn't she just leave it?"

"That's how she keeps her pups clean. In the wild, that helps prevent the spread of parasites and disease."

"Oh, now I'm beginning to understand."

"The pups also dribble urine whenever their mother disciplines them; that shows they recognize her authority. As they get older, they continue this behavior with strange dogs or bigger and stronger littermates for the same reason. You remember what a shy little pup Christi was; every pup in her litter dominated her."

"Gosh, I forgot all about that."

From this conversation Sherry learns that dogs normally urinate to communicate. Although the information helps her understand Christi's reaction to other dogs, does it explain her response to people? Sherry calls the veterinarian to find out. The vet assures her that dogs often react to people the way they do to other dogs. "Christi thinks of you and your company as part of her pack. Because she's unsure of herself, she sees herself as a subordinate member of that pack and pees to show respect." The vet goes on to say that Christi's hearing is so much more sensitive than her owners' that yelling and baby talk make her equally unsure of herself because both sounds are alien to normal dog communication. Furthermore, she cringes when Tim raises his hand or a newspaper because her vision doesn't detect detail well. Almost any quick motion makes her think she's about to get hit.

What about the carpet? Sherry learns from a friend that she can remove the existing stains and odors by soaking the spots in a strong salt solution, vacuuming up the residual salt after the rug dries. Another friend recommends a mixture of white vinegar and water to remove the stains. After the area dries, Sherry can sprinkle a thin layer of moth flakes on the area to further deodorize it and repel the dog. (Although both methods work, proponents of both recommend spot-testing an area to be sure the material is colorfast.) Because of the sentimental and financial value of the rug, Tim doesn't want to take any chances with it, so he consults an Oriental rug dealer and is delighted to discover the firm specializes in the care, cleaning, and storage of valuable carpets. Tim determines how much it will cost to have the rug professionally cleaned and stored.

Step Five: Select and Implement the Best Solution[s]

If you collect sufficient information, learning all you can about the problem, the best solution practically selects itself. To see how this works, let's put together all the information the Bardwells collected about Christi's behavior. Because Christi dribbles urine under several different conditions, wouldn't it be best if we could find a solution that applies to as many of them as possible? That way, whenever Christi confronts those circumstances, she'll experience consistent human responses. Similarly, every time people encounter Christi's dribbling, they can respond consistently. Not only would Tim and Sherry find it easier to fit a minimum number of changes into their busy schedules, their pet would benefit from minimum changes in human behavior. Therefore, the Bardwells decide it's much simpler and effective to tell *everybody* to ignore the dog when they enter the apartment.

Sherry sums up the solutions to the problem so far. "I'll stop the baby talk, you stop the yelling and hitting, and we'll have everyone ignore her when they come in. Even if she pees on the rug."

"Isn't ignoring her cruel, Sherry?"

"Remember, she only pees when people first arrive. After they've been here for a while, she settles down and doesn't make a mistake unless something excites or frightens her. I'm sure our friends will go along with it. After all, they love Chris as much as we do."

"What about her peeing around other dogs? We can't make them ignore her."

"No, but the breeder thinks they'll soon work that out for themselves, especially if we initially restrict canine visitors to the easygoing ones. They can meet in the yard at first, so we don't have the mess in the house."

"And what about the carpet?"

"Let's have it cleaned and stored for a while. I'd rather mop up a bare floor, and you won't have to worry about the rug all the time."

Finally Tim and Sherry can initiate some changes. At first, they both find changing their own behavior more difficult than they had imagined because Tim's *normal* way of letting off steam is to shout, and Sherry's baby talk fulfills her *normal* need. And both Bardwells find it hard to ignore Christi's joyous greetings. Still, their love for the dog makes them try especially hard to adhere to the changes.

In addition to changing their own behavior, Tim and Sherry must also convince any guests to alter theirs.

Friends with dominant dogs are tactfully asked to leave their pets at home for the time being, and those who shared enthusiastic welcomes with Christi are encouraged to ignore the dog. Fortunately, as they hoped, their friends quickly agree because they, too, now understand Christi's behavior and want to see her in a happy relationship with her owners. All the Bardwells' research pays off in more ways than one: soon Tim and Sherry experience a growing confidence in their solutions, a confidence which itself goes a long way toward solving the problem.

Step Six: Evaluate the Results

After a month of consistently adhering to their program, the Bardwells set aside time to evaluate the results.

"It's been two weeks since Christi's peed when we come home," Tim notes, looking at the calendar. Like many owners, Tim finds it helpful to keep track of progress on paper. Using the simple notations T, S, P, and D, he's recorded whenever Christi urinates in his (T), Sherry's (S), other peoples' (P), or other dogs' (D) presence. Interestingly, Christi's record displays no S's or P's during the past week, and fewer T's and D's than before.

Sherry explains that to Tim by saying, "Chris was such a shy pup, I think she's bound to take longer to accept you and other dogs without feeling the need to show submission."

Because it takes time to solve any behavioral problem, we must be patient, tracking results and maintaining a consistent effort over a period of weeks or even months.

However, if the problem persists after a reasonable amount of consistent effort and time, reevaluate the procedure and consider another solution. Did you miss something the first time around? Not surprisingly, this most often happens when the owner collects too little information. Problem analysis and information collection seldom takes more than a day or two; but an inappropriate solution to a poorly defined problem can waste months of your time, and cause even more problems with your dog. Had Tim and Sherry hastily decided to simply lock Christi in a closet when friends arrived or when they went to work, they might have ended up with a howler as well as a dribbler.

The 100 Percent Solution

In this chapter we've seen two typical dog owners progress from a state of almost constant frustration with their dog and themselves to one of increased sensitivity and confidence. At the same time, their dog has transformed from a submissive, nervous wreck into a reliable, confident pet. Both parties achieved more effective communication, eliminating a deteriorating situation in which negative behavior simply created more negative behavior.

Let's review the six-step procedure we'll be using to solve problems in upcoming chapters:

Step One: Recognize the existing behavior as normal.
Step Two: Define the problem.
Step Three: List all possible solutions.
Step Four: Collect information.
Step Five: Select and implement the best solutions.
Step Six: Evaluate the results.

These steps work for any problem, but no formula can succeed without patience and confidence—patience which comes from awareness that effective communication takes time and effort, and confidence that the results of your effort will be a richer, more rewarding relationship with your dog.

Now let's explore each one of the human and canine senses individually and learn to solve problems related to those senses. Then we'll learn how to tackle some more complex problem behavior involving all the senses and see how our new understanding of communication can help us unravel and solve them, too.

Part II
Creating the Invisible Leash-- Sense by Sense

Solid-State Stereo with Your Dog

Svenson Igor, the Hanff's Norwegian elkhound, hasn't been able to adjust to his owners' hectic household. With teenage daughters, there's always rock music blaring, phones ringing, and doors slamming. Although the Hanffs bought the pup over a month ago, he still barks, urinates, or hides under the couch when he hears certain noises.

"Sven, Sven, Sven," Mr. Hanff scolds as he watches the pup scurry behind the couch at the sound of the rustling newspaper. "That pup's scared of his own shadow. I thought elkhounds were supposed to be brave!"

"Maybe he'll outgrow it, Dad," offers the eldest Hanff daughter, Bonnie, as she tries unsuccessfully to grab the terrified pup.

The youngest, Lisa, chimes in, "I bet someone mistreated him before we got him."

"Maybe," replies her mother. "But I won't stand for any growling or snapping. There're too many kids in and out of this house and too much noise to have a fraidy-cat instead of a dog."

Sensing their parents' doubts about keeping Sven, Bonnie and Lisa decide to cure him of his fears. To do so, Bonnie sits and cuddles the pup, while Lisa makes loud noises with pan lids. When the pup tries to break away, Bonnie clutches him tightly, all the while whispering in his ear.

"Shhhhh, shhhhhh, Svenny. It's all right." But the pup only struggles more, causing Bonnie to lose her temper. "Stop it, Svenny, stop it!" she yells, grabbing him by his collar and squeezing him even harder.

The terrified pup leaps wildly, leaving nasty scratches on Bonnie's arm with his needle-sharp claws.

"Maybe Mom's right," Bonnie concedes, massaging her wounds. "Svenny's a chicken."

This brief story illustrates a communication breakdown caused by the dramatic differences between human and canine reception and perception of sound. Not only do sensitive canine ears pick up a greater range of sounds, they display three other characteristics which can lead to miscommunication:

- They don't interpret sounds the same way we do.
- Their sense of touch overrides the sense of hearing.
- Many dogs tend to mimic people.

Unfortunately, many owners assume their dogs hear *better* than they do, but that's not necessarily the case. Let's examine each characteristic of canine hearing and see if we can help the Hanffs develop better communication with Sven.

Orientation: The How and When of Sound Communication

Suppose I ask you to pick out the sound of one oboe playing the same melody with a group of one hundred oboes.

"Impossible," you say. "I could only pick out one if it were playing something different from the others."

Exactly. Now, suppose I ask you to isolate the sound of one oboe in the hundred-piece oboe section of a twenty-five hundred piece orchestra.

"Be serious! If I can't separate one oboe from another, surely I can't separate one from a whole orchestra!"

Obvious? Sure; but we create similar dilemmas for our dogs every day. Just because our dogs can hear many more sounds than we can, doesn't mean they can isolate or distinguish them all, or even the same ones we do. What would it take for one oboist out of a hundred to gain our attention? She might hit a sour note, or she might play a different tune. To alert our dogs, we have to do pretty much the same thing; we must gain their attention—orient them—before we can communicate with them. And *how* we orient them greatly affects the kind of response we get.

The most common way to orient a dog is by using its name. However, most owners quickly develop all sorts of pet names which often so confuse the dog it has no idea what its name is, let alone that it's supposed to pay attention to that name; other owners inadvertently train the dog to ignore its own name by casually dropping it in conversation with others. (Remember Ralphie's owners in Chapter Two?) When the Hanffs really want Sven's attention, they say something like "Svenson Igor, listen up!" whereas the rest of the time they refer to him as Svenny or Sven, or even Dumkopf. Although a dog eventually learns its many pet names, communicating is much easier if owners use only one name or word to get the animal's attention.

Because the Hanffs indiscriminately tossed his name around so often, they soon find Sven ignoring both his name and them. Owners in such a self-created predicament wind up orienting a dog to such negatively charged words as "No!" or "Stop that!" If these words are also used inconsistently, the dog will eventually ignore them too. At this point the frustrated owner believes that the dog is so stupid, only a swat will get its attention, and both dog and owner are trapped in a hard-to-break pattern of miscommunication:

- By indiscriminately using its name, owners train the dog to ignore them.
- Because the dog ignores them, they speak loudly and harshly to it and believe the animal is stupid or spiteful.
- Because the owners speak loudly and angrily to it, the dog becomes confused and fearful of them.
- Because the dog is afraid, it doesn't pay attention to its owner's nonspecific verbal communication; that is, it ignores what the owner is *saying*.
- This reinforces the owner's belief that the dog is stupid and/or spiteful and they hit the dog to gain its attention.

All of this can be avoided simply by training the dog to orient, to pay attention.

If your dog already ignores its name, you can either change its name or pick a word or sound you use only for orientation. Some owners stumble on this technique in anger and learn to orient their dogs with names like Knucklehead, Bonehead, Meathead, Airhead, and Fleabag. These are generally preceded by "Hey," as in "Hey, Bonehead!" Other owners find the "Hey!" alone is sufficient to gain the dog's attention. One of my favorite stories involves a woman who oriented her dog, a delightful Lhasa apso named Chung King, with the name Clarence, in order to solve some behavioral problems. Clarence was her ex-husband's name, a name that she could utter with some force, so she could consistently orient Chung King and distract him from chasing cars.

Although I don't like the implications of communication based on treats, some owners successfully orient their dogs using words like "Cookie?" or "Wanna go for a ride?" Unfortunately, consistently offering such a bribe can lead to the animal ceasing to respond. Whistles, bells, rattling keys, or metal measuring spoons usually work better. Again, be sure to pick a sound that means nothing to the dog except "Pay attention!"

Orienting words work especially well when a lot of other noise (cars, stereos, kids playing) threatens to drown out the communication. If you use your word or sound only when you wish to gain your dog's attention in order to communicate with it, and consistently praise a desired response, your dog quickly learns to listen for it. Although body language and other senses play roles in the overall training process, orienting the animal is a critical first step.

I like to think of the orienting word as the zip code on the envelope of an important letter. Although I have an urgent message inside the envelope, the message may never reach its destination if I don't address it correctly. On the other hand, if I correctly address the envelope but forget to enclose the letter, my correspondent will never receive my message. If I repeatedly make the same mistake, the recipient will begin throwing away the envelopes without even opening them. In summary, orient your dog, send your message, acknowledge the appropriate response.

Hands Off

Even if you successfully use orienting to train your pet, you can lose all the ground you've gained if you touch your dog at the same time. Touch can practically extinguish a dog's hearing. Extinguish? You bet; dogs respond so strongly and defensively to touch, it takes precedence over any sound. Sit in front of your dog, speaking softly to it; then at some point in the conversation, place your hand on its shoulders or pick up a front paw while you continue talking. What happens? Nineteen out of twenty dogs will stop gazing at your face and listening to your words and look at your hand. If your dog views the touch as an expression of dominance, it may even try to pull away or push your hand away. Even if it tolerates your touch, it's obviously more concerned about the pressure of your hand on its body than what you're saying. Even people react this way. Someone's hand on my knee may cause me to see red or hear bells, but I'll hardly remember a thing that person is saying. Or think of a loved one talking about new tires for the car while gently stroking the nape of your neck; how well can you concentrate on his or her discussion of the merits of steel-belted radials?

In addition to pressure, there are two other forms of touch that extinguish a dog's response to sound: a hissing noise and puffs of air. Although you might not consider these forms of physical touch, they may cause a dog to react as strongly as if you hit it. In fact, their effect on a dog's ability or willingness to concentrate on you can be so dramatic, I don't even recommend you try them on your dog to see what happens. Despite the old maxim, "Blow in my ear, and I'll follow you anywhere," this act invariably upsets a dog.

Interestingly, the owner who gives his or her dog the command "Sic 'im!" uses hissing and air puffs, often unknowingly guaranteeing a total fear-based defense response in the animal. Maybe the dog will attack, but it might attack the wrong person, or it might freeze or flee. People who give such commands or make a habit of blowing in or tugging at dog's ears to tease them, create a potentially explosive situation.

A Sound Golden Rule

The third characteristic of canine behavior, mimicry of people, provides a valuable tool for solving many sound-related problems. Suppose you respond to some noise your dog makes by making one yourself. Such exchanges usually escalate something like this:

"Bark, bark, bark, bark."

"Svenny, shut up!"

"Bark, Bark, Bark, Bark!"

"Sven, I said SHUT UP!"

"BARK! BARK! BARK! BARK! BARK!"

"SVENSON IGOR, YOU DUMKOPF. I SAID SHUT UP!!"

Dogs can be tremendous mimics; the more noise we make, the more they make. In the wild, this instinct for imitation enables them to learn survival skills from older animals. Smart owners can use this canine talent to their advantage by adopting a variation of the golden rule: Speak unto your dog as you would have it speak unto you. Remember, when it comes to sound communication with your dog, tone is at least as important as volume and probably more so.

Now let's see how the Hanffs use their knowledge of Sven's hearing to help them solve their problem.

Defusing the Auditory Time Bomb

First, the Hanffs must accept Sven's reaction to noise as normal and overcome their inclination to view his behavior as cowardly, especially for a macho male elk-hound. As you might expect, it's often easier for owners of Yorkies or Chihuahuas than those who own shepherds, Dobermans, or huskies to accept such behavior as normal. If we harbor a strong Rin-Tin-Tin or Nanook of the North image, or if we envision the dog as an extension of our own personality, accepting fear-induced behavior as normal requires a great deal of courage on our parts. On the other hand, continuing to judge the behavior in human terms makes it all the more difficult to alter.

Having accepted the behavior as normal, the Hanffs are ready for step two: defining the problem. Obviously Sven is afraid of noise, but *when* and *why*? The Hanffs quickly realize that the pup reacts more strongly to sudden or unexpected sounds: a motorcycle starting up, Lisa slamming out of the house, a rock station suddenly coming on full blast. However, even if one of these sounds repeats itself, Sven eventually ignores it. After a while the rock music doesn't seem to bother him as much; even if the troublesome sound repeats several hours later, he doesn't respond to it as strongly as he did initially. Putting these observations together, the Hanffs conclude that Sven's behavior stems from his lack of experience and confidence.

But why did the pup respond so viciously to Bonnie's restraint? The deep scratches on Bonnie's arms concern her mother far more than Sven's fear of noises. Is the pup naturally mean? The Hanffs' definition of the *total* problem looks like this:

Problem	*When the Problem Occurs/ Occurred*	*Possible Explanations*
Sven is too easily frightened.	When he hears loud or strange noises.	He's naturally cowardly.
		He lacks experience and confidence.
Sven sometimes attacks.	When he's restrained.	He's mean.
		He's being held incorrectly.
		He doesn't understand why he's being held, due to lack of experience.

Next, the Hanffs confront the Four Basic Options. As often happens within families, they disagree at first. Ms. Hanff wants to send the pup back to the breeder, her husband doesn't really care one way or another because he's not around Sven that much, and both daughters want desperately to keep the dog. In situations like this, the six-step process is a lifesaver because no one has to *do* anything directly with the dog during the first four steps. If the Hanffs immediately enter into some training program that requires all family members' participation, chances are the elder Hanffs would implement it halfheartedly. Without their parents' consistent support, and given the teenagers' incomplete understanding of Sven's behavior, even Bonnie and Lisa might quickly become discouraged with any training program. Enter inconsistency, exit positive results. However, most owners are willing to spend a few hours defining a problem and listing possible solutions. The Hanffs' list of solutions looks like this:

Problem	*Possible Solution(s)*
Sven's too frightened by loud noises.	—Ignore it and hope he outgrows it.
	—Constantly surround him with loud noises.
	—Punish him when he reacts to noises.
	—Gradually accustom him to noise.
	—Get rid of him.

Sven sometimes attacks.

—Ignore the scratches and bites.

—Hang on to him and punish him when he resists.

—Don't restrain him at all.

—Gradually accustom him to being held.

—Get rid of him.

After defining the problem and making this list, the parents decide, in light of their daughters' strong attachment to Sven, to spend a little time collecting information. Besides, Ms. Hanff has gotten interested in the "whys?" underlying Sven's behavior and Mr. Hanff fancies himself the kind of man who can solve *any* problem. As they collect information about the messages loud noises communicate to Sven, they uncover the following facts:

- Sven's hearing is much more sensitive than theirs.
- He was raised in a very quiet kennel, far away from phones, doorbells, kids, or any of the other sounds that are integral parts of the Hanffs' daily life.

These facts help the Hanffs understand why the pup cowers when it hears noises; but do they explain why he attacks anyone who tries to restrain him when he's frightened? Not fully, because both the senses of sound *and* touch have come into play, in tandem and counterproductively, and must be considered. These touch-related facts discussed earlier—that touch instinctively produces a fear response, that touch overrides sound as a stimulus, and that hissing or puffing sounds produce defense responses—shed some light on Sven's resistance to handling.

"I'm not sure I understand," says Bonnie. "If touch overrides sound, why wouldn't my holding Svenny make him forget about the noise?"

"It does," replied her father. "But it makes him think about defending himself—about fighting or escaping—instead. Your holding him just replaces one fear with another."

"When you said 'shhhhh, shhh, Svenny,' you made it even worse," Lisa added. "And when you yelled at him and held him tighter, he went nuts."

By carefully evaluating their information and comparing their human response to sound and touch to Sven's, the Hanffs begin to appreciate how much the pup's world differs from theirs.

"I can understand how he sees things differently, but Sven has to live in our world and nothing excuses him from attacking a child," Ms. Hanff cautions. "What's going to keep him from hurting someone on Halloween or the Fourth of July, when there are a lot of children around?"

In other words, Ms. Hanff has already decided she can't ignore the behavior or hope Sven outgrows it. What are some other solutions?

Because they now know Sven's hearing is much more sensitive and that he was reared in an area with minimal exposure to unexpected sounds, it hardly seems reasonable to punish him for his behavior. Because the Hanffs also know Sven reacts less strongly to sounds he's heard before, constantly surrounding him with loud noises might work. On the other hand, forcing noise on him just might scare him all the more. Similarly, punishing the pup when he responds fearfully to restraint will probably do nothing but increase the response, adding the fear of punishment to his fear of noise. Regardless what the dog fears, it's the fear that manifests itself as unacceptable behavior.

Therefore the best approach to Sven's problem—one which doesn't involve punishment—is to accustom him to different sounds without restraint. The Hanffs can begin with low sounds that don't frighten Sven, and increase the volume of these sounds until they're within the normal range of their household.

Before they began their training program, I suggested the Hanffs teach Sven to orient to a sound other than his name. In this case, I even went so far as to recommend they change Sven's name because of the pup's timid nature and that bothersome hissing "s" sound. When the Hanffs chose the name "Sven" they thought they were communicating his proud Norwegian heritage to their pup, but all the timid pup heard was that threatening hiss.

Following my advice, the Hanffs changed the pup's name to "Thor," after the Norse god of thunder, a joke about his bravery that made the family laugh (remember, humor can improve even the worst situation) and employed a tiny bell sent by Ms. Hanff's mother from Norway to orient the pup. Once Thor began responding to the soft-toned bell, the Hanffs began introducing other sounds one by one at increasingly higher volumes. To make this both easy and fun, Bonnie and Lisa made a cassette tape of the common and not-so-common noises of the Hanff household. They began with fairly common sounds such as slamming doors and dropping pans. Once Thor accepted both the kind of noise and the volume, they progressed to more complex sounds like rock music, sirens, teenage girls shrieking and arguing. Whenever any sound seemed to frighten Thor, the owners quietly oriented and reassured him. In this way the Hanffs were able to control the conditions and respond consistently to them.

Once Thor overcame his fear of sounds, the Hanffs initiated a program to accustom the pup to touch and restraint. At first they limited all petting to the non-threatening zone under Thor's chin and down the front of his chest. As he gained more confidence in himself and his relationship with his owners, he began to take his cues from them rather than his instincts. If the Hanffs weren't afraid of an unusual sound or event, he overcame his instincts to run and hide and remained with them. If they touched him or held him in such a way that instinctively produced a defense response, he learned to recognize what *they* were communicating before he responded. Similarly, the Hanffs learned to appreciate how important their consistency was in helping Thor accept sounds and touches as harmless, or even pleasant, when all his instincts were telling him otherwise.

Using Setups to Prevent Upsets

Any time problem behavior is potentially harmful or embarrassing, setups can be used to decrease these negative effects and speed the training process. A setup involves simulating those situations that usually cause unacceptable behavior so you can deal with them consistently. For example, the Hanffs know Thor will bark frantically at visitors if he can't get away from them, sometimes even threatening to bite—not uncommon behavior in timid pups lacking confidence. Although ignoring the pup stops the behavior, the Hanffs find it difficult to impart that message to the paperboy, their eighty-year-old neighbor, or Ms. Hanff's dog-hating cousin who periodically visits. Under these circumstances, the family can't control the situation consistently enough to stop the barking.

In order to set the pup up, the Hanffs invite friends to visit their home at prearranged times every night for two weeks, making it a game as well as an informative experience for all. Just before the expected arrival time, the Hanffs orient Thor and give a simple command. The instant the doorbell rings, Bonnie says, "Down," fixing Thor with her gaze as she opens the door to let in the visitor; this distracts Thor's attention from the visitor, and forces him to focus on Bonnie. Then, Bonnie lavishly praises the pup for his response to her command, further reinforcing his focus on her. Once the visitor enters, he or she follows Bonnie's instructions to ignore the pup.

Because Thor had developed the bad habit of snapping at some visitors, the Hanffs expanded their setup by telling visitors to repeat the "Down" command *before* Thor's attention drifts to them and he displays aggressive behavior. Because Bonnie had already primed Thor to respond to the command, and because the dog values the positive communication and praise that accompanies successful responses, he willingly obeys. Because it's more difficult for him to attack from a down position, he's more reluctant to do so, and he is forced to consider alternative behaviors.

If the person issuing the command then smiles and responds with the same positive message as Bonnie, it becomes even more difficult for the pup to consider this person a threat. Bonnie and the visitor then alternatively give the pup commands and praise him, until the cause of his original fear loses its meaning.

Thor's snapping resulted from his fear of the unknown based on his lack of experience and self-confidence, so he relied on his primitive defense instincts and when the Hanffs and their visitors responded fearfully to the dog's snapping, that reinforced his belief that a threat existed. By using setups and training (in this case, a consistent response to the "Down" command), they not only boost their own and the pup's self-confidence and open a trusting channel of communication, but they now know how to use set-ups to replace other troublesome tendencies with more acceptable behavior.

Some owners object to setups because they feel they're unfair and manipulative. More projections of human values, I'm afraid. Do dogs experience the same sort of embarrassment people suffer at the hands of others? Hardly. Will a dog feel cheated out of incessant barking, destructive chewing, or car chasing? Unlikely. Once you define setups from your dog's viewpoint, you can once again abandon nonproductive human emotion.

Helping an animal to overcome fear of sound is a lot like teaching it a new language. If the dog responds to a sound as "bad" and we want it to recognize that sound as "good," we must consistently use the sound to mean "good." For example, the Hanffs can't expect Thor to respond nonfearfully to loud noises if they slam pan lids together and smack him any time he misbehaves. On the other hand, if they train him to totally ignore *all* loud sounds, they can't blame him if he ignores any loud sound they *want* him to pay attention to. When we want to teach our animals our language, we have to remember that they're naturally consistent and expect us to be, too.

A Sound Alternative for the Senior Canine

As we go along, we'll discover that most communication problems in young dogs stem from fully functioning senses coupled with too little experience. In older animals, we often see the opposite: the animals have the experience that comes with age, but their sensory apparatus no longer functions at full capacity. Such an animal is often plagued by the same lack of confidence as a young pup. Because they feel vulnerable, geriatric canines may become defensive and want to freeze, fight, or run when they encounter situations that never bothered them before. If owners don't observe the gradually declining senses, they may suddenly find themselves with some knotty problems on their hands.

For example, Ellen Costello first became aware of her eleven-year-old puli's hearing loss when she came home from work one day and found a summons from the dog officer taped to her door. Apparently the beautifully trained, gentle Dulci had bitten the meter reader. How could this be? Faced with a court appearance and feeling a deep sense of responsibility for the safety of those who visit her home, Ellen tackles this problem immediately.

Unemotionally accepting the biting as normal behavior doesn't come easily for Ellen. Feeling guilty and embarrassed, she wonders whether the meter reader did something to make the dog bite. Such an explanation is convenient, but Ellen realizes her pet's biting for whatever reason, under whatever circumstance, is so serious she can't afford to rationalize or ignore it.

Having accomplished step one, Ellen frees herself to concentrate on discovering when and why the biting occurred. The dog officer gives her a copy of the report:

"On January 9, 1984, Joseph Gilliland, an employee of Consolidated Public Service, attempted to enter a residence belonging to Ellen K. Costello at 337 Melody Lane, for the purpose of reading the meter. It was customary for Ms. Costello to leave the back door open for this purpose. On all other occasions Ms. Costello's dog was loose and appeared friendly; it had never threatened Mr. Gilliland in the past. However, on this day the dog was sleeping in front of the back door and when Gilliland tried to step over the dog to enter the house, the dog suddenly jumped up and bit him in the left thigh. The wound required medical treatment, including stitches."

At first Ellen is horrified, angry, and frustrated. "It's just not like Dulci," she mutters. Nevertheless, she calls Mr. Gilliland to apologize and ask him to help her figure out what changed Dulci's behavior so drastically. Ellen's willingness to accept responsibility for what happened quickly reduces Joe's own negative feelings about the incident and he agrees to help.

"Honest, Ms. Costello, I didn't step on her tail or anything. She was sound asleep, and all I did was step over her. She woke up real sudden and bit me."

Weak as it seems, Ellen defines Dulci's problem as "Bites when asleep by back door and someone (stranger) steps over and wakes her." *Why* would Dulci do such a thing? Ellen remembers what Joe said about Dulci waking up suddenly. That sounded strange; Dulci had always been a light sleeper and normally would have heard Joe's footsteps as soon as he entered the yard. Has Dulci suddenly become a sound sleeper? Why didn't she hear Joe's approach?

Considering the Four Basic Options, Ellen decides she can neither accept this behavior nor get rid of the dog. Only if she can't correct Dulci's problem would she consider having her pet put to sleep. Ellen lists other potential solutions:

- Keep Dulci confined at all times.
- Have her thoroughly examined by the vet.
- Post conspicuous "Beware of the Dog" signs on her property.
- Hope it doesn't happen again.

For Ellen, the first two alternatives make the most sense, so she takes Dulci to the vet's, hoping to collect information at the same time. The vet assures Ellen that Dulci is quite normal for her age, but her age does create certain limitations: increased stiffness in hindquarters associated with arthritis, decreased vision caused by changes in the eye structure, and probable hearing loss. Ellen shakes her head. "I guess it's like living with growing children. You don't see the changes. Is Dulci deaf?"

"Not completely, but I suspect there is some loss caused by the deterioration of the nerves and parts of the inner ear which occur with age."

Ellen asks the vet how he can test Dulci's hearing and learns it's not easy to test dogs because they resist restraint and are readily distracted in strange surroundings. However, he does describe ways Ellen may be able to detect a hearing loss at home.

"Try calling her from another room, or snapping your fingers or clapping your hands when she's not looking. If she's lost some of her hearing, she won't respond to familiar sounds if she can't see you. She may also sleep through noises that would have awakened her in the past."

The veterinarian stresses that dogs experiencing gradual hearing loss frequently compensate with vision or other senses. Totally deaf dogs often appear to respond to their owner's call when in fact they're responding to the owner's movement and expression. A woman whose sixteen-year-old spaniel doesn't respond to his name comes immediately when his owner slaps her thighs because he's responding to the motion and perhaps some vibration rather than the sound. Because of this ability to adapt using other senses, a gradual hearing loss may go undetected until something happens to upset the dog's compensating mechanisms.

"I'll be darned," muses Ellen. "Dulci does stay so much closer to me now, she seldom has to depend totally on her hearing for us to communicate. But why would a loss of hearing make her vicious?"

"Although the behavior is hardly acceptable, I wouldn't call it 'vicious.' Dulci awoke suddenly, thought she and your property were being threatened, and responded defensively."

"But she's seen the meter reader before!"

"But this time she was sound asleep and didn't see *or* hear him until he tried to step over her. How would you react if you were hired to protect something but fell asleep on the job, only to wake up with someone hovering over you? You might mistake your own daughter for a burglar and react accordingly."

The simple tests recommended by the vet prove Dulci's hearing has indeed deteriorated. Now Ellen adds "hearing loss" to her definition of the problem, creating other possible solutions:

- corrective surgery
- hearing aid
- training to improve remaining hearing
- using something other than sound to communicate with Dulci

Unfortunately, corrective surgery can't overcome a normal degenerative process associated with aging. Similarly, although Ellen suspects someone has probably invented a canine hearing aid, she considers such an alternative too artificial. Because both remaining possibilities require some form of training, she calls a professional trainer for more information.

The trainer suggests that Ellen train Dulci to respond to cues other than sound, such as flashing lights, scents, or body language. Ellen learns she can use motion to orient Dulci as well as the vibrations created when she stamps her foot. These measures may help Ellen communicate with her dog, but what about other people?

"That's a real tough question to answer, Ms. Costello. You're going to have to watch her closely. Old dogs sleep a lot and sometimes we even forget they're lying behind the rose bush until the little girl next door reaches back there for her ball. Dulci may not be a mean dog, but you'd be doing everyone a favor if you post warning signs on your property."

With his additional information, Ellen reviews her solutions again. According to the veterinarian and the trainer, no matter what she does to compensate for Dulci's loss of hearing, the problem will not go away. On the other hand, Dulci doesn't mind staying in the house while Ellen is at work, and she's content to sleep in Ellen's closed bedroom when Ellen has company.

Ellen implements her chosen changes, and Dulci quickly learns to orient when Ellen stamps her foot. At night, Ellen "calls" Dulci by flashing the porch light. However, Ellen only permits the dog to run free in the small fenced backyard; the rest of the time she keeps the dog on a leash, in close sight, or in a secure room. Ellen also tries to control those conditions that might startle the dog, forewarning her pet gently with her orienting foot stamp. Although the vibrations do startle the sleeping Dulci, the dog associates them with Ellen and doesn't become so frightened and defensive. The result? Ellen and Dulci enjoy a year free from any negative incidents.

Then one morning Ellen receives a letter from her son who's been stationed in Germany with his wife and three young children for the past two years. "I'm being discharged in two months. Can we stay with you for a couple of weeks?" Of course they can, but what about Dulci? Can her son's family learn to compensate for the dog's deteriorating senses or will one of them get hurt?

Ellen's predicament reflects a hard truth about degenerative problems in older dogs: although we can compensate to maintain a quality life-style for ourselves and our pets, that life-style becomes more and more restrictive as time goes by. As interspecies communication grows more and more idiosyncratic and specialized as our animals grow older, as we create a special "language" to talk to our dogs, we make it increasingly difficult to incorporate other people into our life-styles. However, Ellen's ability to confront problems and collect information ensures that any decision she makes will be well thought out and reflect both her own needs and her love of her pet.

Dealing with Deafness

In addition to the gradual deafness associated with aging, dogs can experience deafness or decreased hearing as a result of:

• congenital or hereditary defects
• severe or chronic ear infections
• trauma, such as a blow to the ear or head

In many ways, total deafness or a *fixed* hearing deficit in a younger animal is easier to handle than a gradual loss in an older one. However, different people deal differently with disabilities or handicaps. When Al Shaeffer learns his dog is deaf, he has it put to sleep immediately. Al owns a health spa and centers his entire life around the quest for physical perfection; he simply can't accept owning a "defective" pet. Heartless? Cruel? There are many who would say Al has more of a problem than his dog. Because he obviously can't change the dog's condition or accept it, however, what other choice makes sense? Can Al enjoy a rewarding relationship with an animal who is a constant reminder of the one thing Al fears most: physical imperfection? Sure, those of us with different orientations can blame the Als of this world and say they *could* change, they should *want* to change and become more accepting of these conditions; but relationships based on guilt seldom benefit anyone. How long before that guilt turns (and it invariably does turn) to resentment?

On the other hand, Florence Damico responds in a completely different way to her poodle pup, Clouseau's, deafness. Although the pup is perfectly healthy and normal otherwise, Florence treats Clouseau as though he were a total invalid.

"Poor, poor, deaf baby," she coos, constantly reminding herself and everyone around her of Clouseau's "problem." Rather than use training methods that don't require sound, Florence doesn't train the pup at all. Because she defines him as handicapped and vulnerable, she keeps him indoors most of the time. Consequently, the pup experiences so little, he's extremely shy and fearful whenever company visits, or when Florence leaves him alone. The dog's behavior reflects his owner's belief that he needs her constant protection and care, thereby creating an unproductive cycle. By defining Clouseau's permanent condition as abnormal and requiring major sacrifices on her part, Florence has made the dog totally dependent on her; she's tied herself down to him, and the situation will never improve. All she gets for her loving concern is an unhousebroken, untrained, fearful pet.

Wouldn't it be better if Florence defined Clouseau's world as different rather than deficient? Then she could take heart from the fact that her capacity to communicate with her pet has been changed, not decreased by one fifth.

These two orientations are summed up very well by the biblical verse, " The Lord giveth, and the Lord taketh away." To some, like Florence, this means we each only have so much and if we lose it, it's gone. For others, it means that when one thing is taken away, something else replaces it. For deaf dogs and their owners, life need not mean making the most of a bad deal. It can be a life where the other senses expand to fill the gap left by the loss of hearing and where the animal is no less whole.

Let's take a look at how the Eastabrooks confront the problem of deafness in their Dalmation pup, Alexander. As they ponder the Four Basic Options the family realizes:

- They must accept Alexander's problem because it isn't going to change.
- They want to change any negative feelings they have about deafness into positive ones.
- They must use their more positive feelings to change their behavior toward the dog and employ different methods to train him.
- They don't want to get rid of the pup.

Unlike the Hanffs' problems with Sven, the Eastabrooks face a basic people problem. They have no complaints about the pup's behavior; they just have a problem defining Alexander's deafness, and any changes it necessitates, as "normal" for them.

In the Eastabrooks' case, family discussions about handicaps in general and deafness in particular offer the best source of information regarding changing those feelings. Because they all want to keep the pup, they support each other during this period of learning and change.

Once the Eastabrooks are comfortable with their feelings, they learn about training using hand signals, light, and vibration. Rather than orienting the pup with a sound, they use a white handkerchief and a sweeping hand signal; at night they use a flashlight to duplicate the sweeping gesture. Although they'd prefer to use less noticeable motion, their awareness of the pup's sensitive response to movement makes them realize they need a motion that takes precedence over flying birds, running neighborhood children, bicycles, cars, and so on. Once they have Alexander's attention, they use standard training methods employing hand signals to teach him to come, sit, and stay. If the dog has his back to them, they stamp their feet to orient him with vibrations. Because both owners and dog are learning a new form of communication, it takes a little longer; but Alexander is an eager pupil and the Eastabrooks remember the importance of consistency.

There are moments of frustration, like when Alexander chews up the jacket of Randy's favorite record album and the teenager automatically raises his hand to swat the pup. However, recognizing the pup's immediate attentive response to the gesture, Randy freezes, controls his anger, and gives the pup the signal to sit instead. Each time pup and owner respond consistently, their understanding and ability to communicate with each other and their confidence increase.

Does it bother you that the Eastabrooks seem to have no way to punish Alexander for misbehavior? In the next chapter we'll take a look at punishment as well as some of the other forms of touch that can lead to miscommunication. How would you react if your perfect pup suddenly began terrorizing your six-year-old daughter? Let's see how the Schindlers resolve this and some other touchy problems.

Mounting, Pawing, Clawing and Other Touchy Problems

Before Howie and Gale Weisbuch bred their vizslas, they learned all they could about that particular breed and dog care in general; then they carefully selected a male and female, trained them, and painstakingly cared for them. All their efforts paid off when Katrinka gave birth to five healthy pups with no problems whatsoever. The Weisbuchs were ecstatic, as were their friends who eagerly laid claim to the wonderful offspring.

One of the pups went to the Weisbuchs' close friends, Evan and Debbie Schindler, who hadn't seriously considered owning a dog until they saw these exceptional canines. The Schindlers chose an exuberant male and left the Weisbuchs' home filled with dreams of all the happy times they'd share with their wriggling bundle of fur.

A month later, barely able to control her anger and

frustration, Debbie Schindler called Gale to complain, "That damn pup mounts everything in sight. It's disgusting!"

Gale was shocked. "He can't be! He's much too young!"

"Well, he is. He's constantly bothering Kimmy when she's playing on the floor, and gets worse every day. If this keeps up, I'm going to bring him back."

In the preceding chapters we discussed how sound or touch can cause certain canine problems because they elicit defensive responses. From the beginning of our relationship, we owners and our dogs react to touch in radically different ways. To humans, touch signifies an *intimate* expression. If we hug or caress someone, we do so to display fondness. If we smack an errant child's rump or slug a human octopus in a single's bar, we do so to express disapproval. In other words, like so many of our sensual perceptions, we humans attach a wide range of values to different forms of touching from the best to the worst. As a rule we don't casually hug and kiss strangers, nor do we randomly slug passersby on our way to the supermarket.

Not only do people hold strong feelings about touching or being touched by other humans, many of us harbor strong interspecies touch-related prejudices, too. Do you remember the Peanuts cartoon in which Lucy reacts to Snoopy's kisses by recoiling and yelling, "Argghhh, I've been kissed by a dog!"? Or imagine the horrified look on the face of the nondog-owning new mother who watches a lovable Newfoundland try to spruce up Junior with a few sloppy licks. "Yuck," she thinks, "germs!"

On the other hand, compare our intricate human interpretations of touch to the dog's. Whether a dog lives in a penthouse in Paris or a tenement in a Baltimore slum, it naturally responds to touch in one of three ways: fight, freeze, or flee. And like all instinctive behaviors, the responses occur and cause problems most frequently in young pups. Until experience teaches them otherwise, immature animals rely heavily on their instincts. Let's see how the disparity between human and canine interpretation of touch turned the Schindlers' dream pup into a nightmare.

The Canine Mounty

When Evan and Debbie Schindler decided to take one of the Weisbuchs' pups, they made the selection a family affair. Packing their ten- and six-year-old children, Justin and Kimmy, into the car, they headed for the Weisbuchs' to take their pick of the litter. When the family first saw the pups, mayhem broke loose. Kids screamed, puppies yelped excitedly, and everybody worked themselves into a frenzy. Amid the oohs, ahhs, and giggles, the Schindlers were captivated by a bouncy male, the liveliest pup of the litter.

"We want this one!" crowed the children as they ran around and around with the pup, and Quabbin immediately became a member of the Schindler household.

Unfortunately, in the four short weeks Quabbin has lived with the Schindlers, the relationship has soured. When Kimmy sits on the floor, Quabbin puts his front paws on her shoulders or back, sometimes with enough force to topple her over. This so upsets Kimmy, she has begun to avoid the pup, and her mother senses Kimmy's growing fear of the dog. On the other hand, both Justin and his father encourage Quabbin's rough-and-tumble play by getting down on all fours and chasing the pup around and around the house. When they catch him, they flip him over on his back and "tickle" him. The few times Kimmy tried to join in this game, Quabbin growled and nipped her with his needle-sharp baby teeth.

"I don't like the way that pup picks on Kimmy, Evan," Debbie says with a frown. "He's always after her, and he acts so horny."

"Oh, don't be such a prude. Kimmy's so timid, she lets him get away with it. She's got to learn how to play rougher."

"I don't agree; I don't like the way Quabbin intimidates her. It's not right."

"Stop babying her," counters Evan. "I'll teach her to be more forceful."

"Yeah, Mom," Justin chimes in. "Quabbin's a super pup. Kimmy's just a scaredy-cat."

Then one day Deb found Kimmy pinned down by the dog, and she immediately called Gale Weisbuch.

A very touchy situation. First of all, half the family (Justin and Evan) wouldn't change the pup, whereas the other half (Kimmy and Deb) wish they'd never gotten a dog. Turning to our six-step problem-solving process, can we define such a situation as normal? If Quabbin is "wrong," so are Justin and Evan. If Quabbin is "right," Kimmy and Deb have a problem.

This sort of conflict often arises in families, especially when the dog becomes a means for family members to assert their own beliefs. If their beliefs differ sufficiently, they have a hard time defining and solving any problem. Where to begin? When a family holds two different ideas of what constitutes a good relationship with a pet, their inconsistent definitions of acceptable or negative behavior make consistent communication with the dog impossible. To overcome this, the Schindlers might think of their differing opinions as two opposing armies squaring off on a battlefield with Quabbin in the middle. Then they can see how, regardless of which side wins, the pup is bound to get hurt.

Another way the Schindlers might more easily define Quabbin's behavior as normal is to first review the Four Basic Options. If they decide they want to keep the dog, something has to change. If they all want to keep the pup, they should be willing to make changes, even if the first changes means relinquishing personally favored, but unhelpful, value judgments. Even though Evan and Deb strongly disagree over the acceptability and meaning of Quabbin's behavior toward Kimmy, they can only achieve a happier relationship with each other and the dog if they try to understand each other's point of view.

Having accomplished that, the Schindlers must now sort through that bewildering mixture of human and canine behavior to define the problem. Evan and Deb construct their problem list with as little emotion and judgment as possible:

Problem	When the Problem Occurs/ Occurred	Possible Explanations
Quabbin bothers and frightens Kimmy.	Whenever he can, but mostly when she sits on the floor.	He's playing.
		Justin encourages him to play rough.
		He wants to hurt her.
		She lets him do it.

Evan and Justin play too rough with Quabbin.	All the time.	That's how pups like to play.
		To make him excited.
		To keep him from becoming a sissy.
		To show him who's boss.
Kimmy doesn't handle Quabbin forcefully.	All the time.	She's afraid of him.
		She's too gentle.
		He's too aggressive.

Before we look at alternative solutions, let's help the Schindlers determine the senses involved in each part of the problem.

When the pup jumps up on Kimmy, seemingly without provocation, *touch* obviously comes into play. Notice how Evan and Deb describe both types of problems with the pup in terms of touch: male play is rough, whereas Kimmy's is gentle. Immediately Deb and Evan decide to find out more about Quabbin's sense of touch.

In this case, information collection helps the owners exchange the emotional arena, where personal opinion causes conflict, for that of objective research. Their friends and Quabbin's breeders, the Weisbuchs, agree to sit down with the family one Saturday afternoon to see if their knowledge of dogs in general and vizslas in particular might shed some light on the problem.

Gale Weisbuch explains that mounting behavior doesn't always have a sexual meaning. "Puppies often use it to establish their pack or social order. Even dogs of the same sex will mount each other for this purpose."

Like so many owners, it takes the Schindlers some time to come to grips with the fact that touch means something distinctly nonhuman to Quabbin. Not only does touch elicit his defense response, certain touches in certain areas deliver specific messages. For example, in the struggle to establish pack hierarchy, touch or pressure in the shoulder area asserts dominance. "If a dog stands on its hind legs and places its front paws on the shoulders of another, the underdog may go down and roll on its back, signifying its acceptance of the other's authority. If, on the other hand, the underdog feels it's the more dominant, it may fight."

Remember how dogs incorporate people into the pack structure? Let's analyze Quabbin's responses to touch to learn how the pup views the Schindler pack. When Evan and Justin flip Quabbin over on his back, they're expressing dominance, so Quabbin reacts submissively. On the other hand, when the pup jumps up on Kimmy and knocks her over, he's obviously expressing his own dominance over a pack member he sees as submissive. So where does Deb fit in?

"Well, he tried to jump up on me a couple of times, but when I grabbed him by the scruff of the neck and shook him, he quit."

Although Quabbin attempted to dominate Deb at first, he quickly learned to recognize her as dominant, too. This, in addition to her adult size which the young pup also recognizes, places her below Evan, but above Justin in the pack hierarchy. So Quabbin sees the order of the Schindler pack in terms of dominance like this: Evan, Deb, Justin, Quabbin and, least dominant of all, Kimmy. Armed with their new understanding, Evan and Deb feel confident as they list possible solutions:

Problem	*Possible Solution(s)*
Quabbin bothers and frightens Kimmy.	—Teach Kimmy to stop him.
	—Discipline him every time we catch him.
	—Ignore the behavior.
Evan and Justin play rough with Quabbin.	—Change the kind of play.
	—Tone down all play.
	—Teach Quabbin to respond differently to the play.
	—Stop all play.
Kimmy doesn't handle Quabbin forcefully.	—Teach Kimmy to be firmer with the pup.
	—Have Kimmy engage him in the same rough play as Evan and Justin.
	—Teach Quabbin to respond to Kimmy as a dominant figure.
	—Keep Kimmy away from Quabbin.

As they examine their alternate solutions, the Schindlers decide they want to create a relationship with Quabbin in which he recognizes everyone in the family as dominant, but not threatening. Although Quabbin views all but Kimmy as dominant, this pack order came about rather haphazardly. Wouldn't it be much better to establish dominance through training? Because they admire the behavior of Quabbin's parents so much, they again ask the Weisbuchs for advice.

"I'm glad you asked," says Howie. "Even though this particular line of vizslas has been bred for a soft mouth and rarely bites, you remember that Quabbin was the largest and most active pup in the litter. He dominated all the others. In fact, Gale and I worried about giving him to you because such a pup needs especially thoughtful training."

"We never thought of that. Should we have taken a smaller female?"

"Perhaps, but a more submissive pup can pose other problems, such as shyness or dribbling urine at the slightest provocation."

Howie goes on to recommend they tone down the roughhousing and involve the whole family in simple training procedures. Because Kimmy is too small to use force effectively, Howie suggests they distract the pup from negative behavior.

"After all," notes Howie, "Kimmy needs a method that'll work when she's alone with Quabbin."

Howie gives them a small can of pennies, advising the family to shake it *only* when they want Quabbin's attention. He also shows both adults how to put the pup in the submissive "belly-up" position whenever he gets too pushy or dominant.

"Flip the pup on his side, then hang on to the legs

closest to the ground or floor so he can't get up. Place your arm across his neck so he can't bite. You can practice this technique when Quabbin is lying quietly until you master it." He adds a warning that, although this position (also called the alpha roll) works very well with pups like Quabbin, it could elicit a defensive response from an adult dog.

Parents of young children find the alpha roll a valuable aid when pup and kids start working themselves into a frenzy. Every parent recognizes the increased pitch of excited voices and the accelerated pace of activity that invariably precedes a shattered lamp or nip on the ear. Send the kids to their rooms for a little quiet time, then hold the pup in the alpha position until it settles down. Bear in mind that when pups and children get together, even normally quiet animals may need some calming down.

After talking to Howie, the Schindlers decide to replace their random and conflicting play routines with a new one: consistent training. Because they recognize that the hissing "s" sound provokes defensive reactions, they decide to teach Quabbin to respond to the command "Down" rather than "Sit."

During the next month, the family sets aside two ten-minute periods every day to work with the pup. At first parents and children train Quabbin together, but gradually Justin and Kimmy begin conducting their own sessions. Realizing the value of consistency, Evan and Deb make the sessions as much a part of the family routine as mealtimes and bedtime stories. They also forbid physical punishment and loud words, insisting that everyone use the distracting penny can instead. At first Justin resists these restrictions, but when he understands Kimmy must be able to employ the same technique to avoid confusing Quabbin, he finds it easier to comply. Deb also finds that having Justin teach Kimmy helps her son consistently train the dog.

At the end of the month, the Schindlers hold a family conference to evaluate their progress.

"Gee, Mom," Justin comments, "when you said I had to teach Quabbin and Kimmy, I thought it would be boring, just like school. But this is really fun."

Deb smiles. "How about you, Kimmy? How do you feel about Quabbin now?"

"He listens to me almost all the time, and never jumps on me like he used to," Kimmy offers eagerly.

"Can we teach Quabbin some tricks?" Justin interrupts.

"Sure, why not? The Weisbuchs say our training techniques can teach Quabbin all sorts of things."

The whole family benefits from their ability to apply their new communication skills to other areas, and Quabbin develops into an adult dog worthy of his prize-winning parents.

Keeping in Touch with Changing Needs

Remember, miscommunication with pups often results from a combination of the pup's fully developed senses and relatively limited experience, whereas problems with aging animals often result from increased sensitivity to touch combined with a gradual loss of their full range of perception. Why is touch the exception to the rule? Because while other senses may deteriorate, many aging animals may develop physical conditions that are aggravated by touch. Although this continued awareness of touch serves a protective function, it can become exaggerated and problematic.

When Irene and Lydia Ustinov's borzoi, Anastasia, began to age, her decreased vision and hearing troubled her owners less than her tendency to snap whenever anyone touched her. The sisters felt they could cope with a blind or deaf dog, but not a biting one. As expected, recognizing the existing behavior as normal posed the most difficulty. One day in exasperation, Irene turned to Lydia and shouted, "Anastasia shouldn't be biting people. Maybe we'd just better get rid of her!" Lydia broke down sobbing.

Such a shocking verbalization of the irreversible solution jolted the sisters out of nonproductive musing about poor old Anastasia, and they soon realized they had been projecting their own fears of growing old on the dog. Such fears, however real to us, make it difficult to solve problems.

When Lydia and Irene confront the Four Basic Options, they realize they can't accept Anastasia's behavior or change the negative way they feel about it. They're not sure whether Anastasia can change at this age or whether there's anything they can do to help her, and yet they would hate to get rid of her.

Most owners of older dogs gradually confront this dilemma: do we put the old dog to sleep, or do we wait until something terrible—incapacitating illness or a bitten child—takes the choice out of our hands? Each day negative behavior resulting from the pet's deteriorating condition persists, whittling away fond memories of a previously rewarding relationship. We've all heard tales

of once excellent athletes who were so proud they kept
trying to perform beyond their prime, often ruining the
great reputation they created, and alienating those who
faithfully supported them over the years. The same thing
often happens with dogs; we create a very good relationship together, but we wake up one day to realize the
dog no longer maintains its end of the bargain. We
feel cheated and frustrated. Yet unlike the athlete
who must simply confront retirement, our dogs force
us to confront life's inevitable ultimatum: death and
euthanasia.

Fortunately, our six-step procedure helps remove much
of the fear and emotion that often attends problems in
older animals, thereby reducing the chances of encoun-
tering the crushing doubt and guilt that can accompany
a hasty decision. Lydia and Irene construct a problem
list that looks like this:

Problem	When the Problem Occurs/Occurred	Possible Explanations
Anastasia bites.	When she's touched.	She's afraid.
		She hurts some-where.
		She's senile.
		She's mean.

Considering the possible explanations for Anastasia's
behavior, Lydia and Irene come up with various solutions:

Problem	*Possible Solution(s)*
Anastasia bites when she's touched.	—If she snaps because of pain, remove the pain.
	—If she snaps because she's afraid, eliminate her fears.
	—Observe and control her at all times.
	—Keep her away from others.

Because the possibility of removing pain seems the most hopeful, the Ustinovs take Anastasia to the veterinarian for a thorough examination, during which they learn the dog is suffering from arthritis in both her shoulders and hips. The vet assures them that medication relieves the discomfort to some degree in most dogs. He also stresses the importance of consistent exercise and sound footing.

"Don't let her lie around all week and then take her for a long-walk on Sunday afternoon. She'll really suffer on Monday morning. And dogs rely on sound footing, especially for their back legs, to feel secure. Even a dog with good hips feels vulnerable on unsure footing, just like you feel trying to navigate on ice. Your hardwood or vinyl floors are just alike a skating rink for an old dog with joints like Anastasia's, so try to keep her on carpet or grass as much as possible."

When Lydia asks if Anastasia's arthritis could cause her to snap, the vet nods.

"But it's not just the discomfort itself; it's how that discomfort arises. When someone touches her shoulders or paws, they're signaling dominance, telling Anastasia that that person wants a confrontation. Because she's so attached to you, Anastasia will let you get away with this, but it elicits her defensive instinct to protect your household if someone else does it. Furthermore, because dogs need their rear ends firmly planted to defend themselves or their property effectively, a stranger's touch on Anastasia's hips poses a double threat. The pain itself makes her defensive, and it threatens the very position she needs to make an effective defense response."

"Will medication cure her problem?"

"If we can block the discomfort long enough for Anastasia to disassociate her pain from the act of being touched, we might be able to reduce her fears of human contact."

The vet goes on to explain that dogs are conditioned-response animals: if they experience the same sequence of events every time a set of conditions arises, they learn to anticipate the entire sequence. For example, in a famous experiment, Pavlov rang a bell before he fed his dogs. After a while he noticed the dogs began salivating as soon as they heard the bell; in the dogs' minds, the bell had gone from a meaningless sound to one that meant food. Anastasia made a similar association between two previously unrelated events. When she sleeps or lies quietly, she forgets her aches and pains, but as soon as someone touches her, especially if the touch startles her, she tenses her limbs and immediately experiences pain. In her mind, the touching caused the pain, so she sees the toucher as the *cause* of her discomfort. By blocking the pain long enough for Anastasia to break this erroneous association, she may more easily adjust to normal aging changes. (Remember, too, that although we use the word *pain*, it doesn't carry all our negative human implications; in dogs, the positive protective sensation of pain helps them adjust to physical limitations without hurting themselves.)

The vet continues to explain how some older animals can actually respond to smaller doses or weaker forms of medication once they realize the discomfort is a normal part of their lives, not an indication of an attack or threat and not related to people.

When Lydia and Irene review their list of possible solutions, they realize that the medication might reduce Anastasia's discomfort *and* her fears. Therefore they decide to try it; however, they also wisely decide to evaluate the situation in three weeks. Although evaluation is a critical step in any problem-solving procedure, many owners find it difficult to place limits on solutions involving medication because they tend to follow the same never-say-die approach that too often characterizes human medicine. Most veterinarians want owners to set limits, even if those limits are "I'll try anything" or "I won't try anything at all." Then the vet can tailor any treatment to the needs of both owner *and* pet.

Sometimes owners want the veterinarian to set limits for them, but that seldom works well, especially in cases such as Anastasia's. When Lydia and Irene evaluate the dog's condition, they must not only evaluate the result of the medication but also their feeling about medicating their pet. If they aren't pleased with either Anastasia's response or their own, they must reevaluate and possibly redefine the problem. Is the problem less an old dog who bites than a beloved family pet that's become a burden?

As we discovered in the last chapter, communication problems with older dogs don't go away, nor do they remain the same. Conditions change constantly and owners can save themselves a lot of headaches and heartaches by evaluating problems on a regular basis. When the Ustinovs evaluate their results, they acknowledge Anastasia's dramatic improvement in both temperament and physical well-being; and they don't mind the hassle of daily medication because it restores a rewarding relationship between them and their dog.

More Touchy Situations

Although people have bred certain types of dogs to heighten their senses of smell, hearing, and vision, they haven't bred more touch-sensitive ones per se. Nevertheless, some groups of dogs are more touchy than others. Dogs of all ages who lack confidence—whether due to a physical limitation such as blindness or deafness, some medical problem such as lameness, or improper training—may react much more strongly to unexpected touch. Similarly, physically normal dogs with submissive personalities may freeze, fight, or flee when touched. To develop rewarding relationships with such dogs, owners must help build confidence with consistent training and communication.

Other touch-related problems arise because some people associate certain forms of touch with affection, whereas others find those same touches in the same, or different, places repulsive. Licking is a fine example. Remember the first time that new ball of fluff licked you with its rough little pink tongue? Did the behavior thrill or disgust you? If you liked it, you may have sought ways to get the pup to repeat it ("Kiss-kiss, give Mummy a kiss, MaiTai."). However, remember dogs expect consistency and have limited detail vision. If it's all right to kiss

Mummy on the lips, MaiTai expects to be able to kiss the dog-hating minister on the lips, too. If MaiTai is also a social sniffer and takes a few slobbering licks at the Avon lady's crotch, we've got even more trouble. Here again, consistency is the key: train the dog to display the behavior you feel is acceptable to you, your family, *and* visitors. To have separate standards is not only confusing, it's also counterproductive. Rather than learning three different responses to the same general conditions, you may find the dog uniformly misbehaving all the time.

Sometimes our dogs teach us to respond to their touch. Do you automatically respond to your dog's licking, nuzzling, pawing, whining, and barking message to "Stop what you're doing and pay attention to me!"? Then you're a well-oriented owner. Unfortunately, many times, this process then deteriorates into a guessing game: "MaiTai want to go out?" "MaiTai want a cookie?" If you reward such behavior, you insure it will continue. And such indiscriminate pawing, whining, barking, and licking can lead to problems such as damaged clothing, complaints from neighbors, and spoiled dinner parties.

If you suspect your dog is communicating dominance rather than affection with its licking, pawing, and so on, simply ignore the behavior and substitute simple commands, using the orient-command-praise sequence. As with so many miscommunication problems, embarrassed or flustered owners may find it difficult to implement any consistent diversion or substitution training in the presence of strangers; so if the dog exhibits unacceptable behavior toward others, use setups.

"So how will Mai Tai be able to tell me she wants to go out, eat, or play ball if I teach her not to bark, scratch, or lick?"

I'm not saying it's wrong to teach a dog to ask for

specific things in a specific way. All I'm saying is be aware of what you're teaching and whether or not it's a behavior that's acceptable to everyone that comes in contact with the dog, and one that can be consistently acknowledged and rewarded. It's no use teaching MaiTai to bark to go out if there's no one there to let her out. Nor can we reward her pawing for food today but say "No, you're too fat" to the same behavior tomorrow, or when a visiting relative finds such begging repulsive.

If you want your dog to paw or lick you to signal a specific desire, merely reinforce *that and only that* behavior under those conditions. Don't take the dog for a walk when he brings his leash, barks at the door, *or* paws your arm. Select just one of those behaviors to mean "I want to go for a walk," and respond only to that one. Although setups are more difficult when we're in essence training the dog to train us, they can be used. For example, you can begin by walking the dog or playing ball with it at the *same* time every day for several weeks. Show the dog the ball or leash as you remove it from a place easily accessible to your pet. When you place the leash on the dog or pick up its ball, orient it and say the appropriate word ("MaiTai, leash," "MaiTai, ball"). Repeat the orientation and word periodically during the walk or play session.

Once the dog expects the outing or play, stall. Remain sitting and pretend to read your paper. When the dog appears agitated or restless, give the command; the dog has already learned the connection from the owner and will automatically get the leash or ball. Obviously, lavish praise is the final step.

What happens if you don't *want* to play ball or go for a walk? When teaching the behavior, it's important you consistently acknowledge the dog's desired response to firmly establish it; once this occurs, your pet's behavior can absorb and even be strengthened by a certain amount of inconsistency. Bear in mind, however, that although inconsistency may perpetuate certain *established* behaviors, it inhibits effective behavioral changes. It also creates a certain amount of frustration and disappointment, which isn't our goal. The goal of training isn't training— it's mutually beneficial communication.

A Hit or a Mess?

In our study of the tactile response and its effect on communication, we've emphasized how touch naturally elicits a defensive response in dogs. But how do we get from the freeze, fight, or flee message to one that means "Don't do that!" "Put that bone down!" "Don't pee on the rug when I'm gone!"? Many owners connect the two with violence.

"It's not the swat that teaches the dog; it's the pain that comes after it." A lot of dog owners believe that the dog experiences the pressure or touch of impact, rejects its natural defense response to freeze, fight, or flee, then concentrates on the pain (which is *not* instinctively negative) as an indication of the owner's displeasure. But does the dog know *why* the owner is upset? Is it something the dog did or didn't do? Is it the way it's walking toward the owner, or the fact that it isn't sitting by the door?

Although I hesitate to insist that all owners abandon physical punishment, I strongly prefer distraction to divert a dog from negative behavior. Because I'm not a large person myself and have raised a big dog with small children underfoot, I realize the foolishness of believing we all have the strength of mind and body to use consistent physical force to discipline our dogs. One of the most pathetic sights I ever saw was a five-foot, hundred-pound woman impotently beating her hundred and fifty pound Saint Bernard with a rolled up newspaper as the animal dragged her down the street, through parking lots, and over fences.

Keep in mind, too, that owners who use physical punishment must be consistent. If Carmine Lucaya swats Ferdie for barking at visitors, then she must swat him every time this occurs. She can't hit him today when his barking drowns out her favorite soap opera, then add her own joyful screams to his barks when her long-lost nephew comes to call tomorrow. Similarly, unless *everyone* who handles the dog can use the same form of discipline, it's not going to work. Maybe Mom can line the kids up for Dad to thrash when he gets home from work, but Fido's memory isn't that good; he won't have the foggiest idea why he's being hit with a rolled newspaper at 5 P.M. for some bad deed done at 7 A.M. More likely the dog will associate the swat with whatever it was doing the moment its owner came toward it: "Boy, am I happy to see you! Look how I'm wagging my tail!" Whap! Soon the dog begins to crouch and cower every time the owner comes home with the *Times* under his arm, and the owner wonders why.

Furthermore, physical punishment doesn't communicate any consistent message except that the owner is angry about something, which may or may not be about what the dog is or isn't doing. Every owner who totes a rolled up newspaper must answer this question: Is punishing the dog more important to me than changing the behavior? Sadly, we dog owners sometimes resort to physical punishment to fulfill our *own* needs rather than the dog's. How many times have you shouted, "Frederick, stop that!" then clapped your hands, effectively getting your dog to stop the behavior, only to go ahead and smack him anyway? My own record with Dufie proves that the use of physical punishment has little to do with the magnitude of a dog's transgressions, but a lot to do with our all-too-human moods. Once, I barely acknowledged that he had shattered a beloved vase; a few days later, I clobbered him for breaking an inexpensive dish I had always hated anyway. Why was I so angry about the dish? Because a bunch of neighborhood kids had tracked mud through the house. An awareness of my own motives and inconsistency coupled with my awareness of canine perception convince me that physical punishment offers such a mixed bag of miscommunication, it ends up communicating nothing worthwhile.

For most owners, the major message they wish to convey via discipline isn't "I want to hurt you," but "Stop that" or "Do this!" Distraction delivers the message beautifully. Owners who train their dogs to respond to an orienting word or sound can use it for distraction as well. I like this method because it keeps things simple. For example, just as Ferdie opens his mouth to give that first yip when the doorbell rings, Carmine says, "Ferdie!" just loudly enough to gain his attention. Then she gives him the command, "Get your ball." When the dog responds, he receives lavish praise. Meanwhile the guests enter the house without the usual canine soundtrack. No pain, no anger; just the replacement of an unwanted behavior with a more acceptable one.

Small cans of pennies or marbles, metal measuring spoons, or bells also make effective distractors. These work especially well in the hands of young children or soft-spoken and unassertive teens and adults who can't get enough pizzazz into their voices to effectively distract (or attract) a dog. Remember, it's not so much a question of volume as one of quality and consistency. Like the orienting word, only use distraction when you mean it. If you rattle the penny can just because you like the sound of it, your dog will soon learn to ignore it and you.

Many owners find training a dog a lot harder than punishing because training requires they control *themselves* as well as the dog. I deliberately distinguish between training and punishing because training with punishment isn't "training" at all. Training means the animal learns to exhibit certain behaviors and not others because it recognizes acceptable ones benefit its relationship with its owner. As we discussed in Chapter One, teaching and learning are expressions of love. I'm not saying consistent use of physical punishment can't produce an obedient dog any more than I'm saying the inconsistent use of distraction can. What I am saying is that when communication is as important as obedience, consistent training with distraction rather than punishment forms a much higher quality relationship between owner and dog.

Now that we've gotten a good feel for touch, let's see if we can make some sense out of scents.

Smell: The Tantalizing Telegram

When Claudia Lehane and Mark Stuckey set off for a picnic in the country with Mark's beagle Beauregard, Claudia had high hopes Mark was finally going to pop the question. While she spread a blanket under a leafy maple in a field of wild flowers and pulled wine, crusty French bread, imported cheeses, fresh fruit, and Swiss chocolate from the picnic hamper, Beauregard raced off to explore the woods. Soon Claudia and Mark settled down for a romantic and memorable afternoon.

It turned out to be too memorable. Just as Mark raised his glass, stared deeply into Claudia's eyes, and opened his mouth to speak, Beauregard bowled into them, caked with cow manure. The same gentle summer breeze that now filled Claudia's nose with barnyard odors had carried the scent of her painstakingly prepared canapés and other delicacies to the dog. Beauregard lunged. Hoping to keep the dog's muddy feet out of the pâté, Claudia caught him midair and clutched him tightly to her lacy bodice. The instant Beauregard caught a whiff of her expensive perfume, he sneezed violently in her face.

"What the hell is going on?" shouted Mark amid the confusion.

That was *not* the question Claudia had hoped to hear.

As with touch, human and canine senses of smell differ so drastically that we must try especially hard to understand the dog's point of view. Just as our dogs hear a greater frequency and range of sounds, and interpret touch in their own special way, so they can detect a wider variety and a lower concentration of odors, interpreting the attendant messages in ways that often repulse their owners. Recognizing what odors *mean* to our dogs can make a huge difference in our relationships with them. As usual, we must figure out what's normal *for them*.

Creating a Scent-sational Picture

Dogs use scent much the way business people use calling cards to announce their names, firms, specialties, addresses, and phone numbers. When dogs want to identify other animals, they collect scent data from that animal's body, creating their basic scent pictures from information gleaned from the other's mouth, rectal, and genital areas. They gather meaningful facts from secretions, waste products, and oozing sores. Does this sound disgusting to you? It's not surprising: our society recoils at even the most natural odors. With all the mouthwashes, deodorants, perfumes, shampoos, soaps, and douches we use, it takes little imagination to understand why we stand so remote from our dogs when it comes to interpreting scent data.

When Beauregard rolls in meadow muffins, he's responding to scent cues that urge him to explore the territory. When he catches a whiff of Claudia's liver pâté and crackers, another set of cues pulls him toward the food. While he explores instinctively, he has also *learned* to respond to the smell of food because his owner has taught him to attach meaning to it. When the dog pursues these cues, his delicate and sensitive olfactory apparatus is assaulted by Claudia's expensive perfume, and he sneezes to rid himself of the irritant, exhibiting yet another characteristic of the canine system.

How does Claudia interpret these same events? With disgust. Obviously she and her boyfriend's dog don't "smell nose to nose."

Although most people readily accept sniffing as normal canine behavior, they may still be horrified when their dog tries to burrow into Aunt Sadie's armpit or Uncle Harry's crotch. They don't see those odor-laden microscopic bits of skin and hair flaking off Sadie and Harry at the rate of about 40,000 each minute; nor do they recognize the dog devotes 10 to 26 times more area to olfactory membranes and almost 10 times more of its brain to interpret the data collected by the membranes. Such differences are often beyond human comprehension. People who can easily accept differences in canine hearing or sight often find it difficult or even impossible to accept their dog's scent-related behavior as normal, especially when it comes to stool. Let's see how our human interpretation of scent messages originating from the dog's most basic bodily secretions can jeopardize our relationships with our pets.

Housebreaking: Winning By a Nose

Harley, Bruce and Jolene Siegal's fourteen-week-old basset hound pup, defecates all over the house.

"I can't stand it," Jolene sighs. "Why does Harley do this to us? Does he hate us that much?"

"I don't think he hates us. Maybe he's just nervous," suggests Bruce.

One evening when Bruce found Harley defecating on the family room rug, he sneaked up behind the unsuspecting pup and swatted him hard. The surprised dog expressed his anal glands, and the combined odors plus the pup's obstinate refusal to acknowledge his owners' wishes so infuriated Bruce, he grabbed the pup by the scruff of the neck and jammed his nose into the mess. When Jolene and her daughter Beth came home an hour later, the house still reeked, the trembling Harley cowered under the couch, and Bruce sat forlornly in his favorite chair.

"I've just about given up on Harley. No matter what we do, he never learns." Bruce shook his head sadly. "This place smells like an outhouse."

The sense of smell figures prominently in housebreaking. Urine and stool appear in boldface type on each dog's calling card, and other dogs immediately zero in on these rich data banks. The dog views these messages less as waste products than as a photograph of the never-seen pen pal a person might take to the airport to help identify her in the crowd. Of course, healthy dogs deposit their urine and stool away from those areas where they eat and sleep, but they don't get hung up on all the emotional meanings people associate with the presence of such substances in certain areas.

In Chapter 3 we observed submissive urination in a pup. Harley, on the other hand, urinates and defecates in the house because he's too young to control the muscles of his bladder and rectum, and because he hasn't been taught otherwise. The circular muscles that control the opening and closing of the rectum and urinary tract develop later in pups than other muscles. Because of this, Harley's owners must pay special attention to *timing* in the early stages of housebreaking; if they can control *when* he urinates and defecates, they can control *where* he does so.

"He's not normal," says Jolene. Oh, oh; watch your step, dear owner, because you must take step one and define Harley's behavior as normal for him *at this time*. Is Harley a horrible dog doing horrible things? No, he's a normal pup behaving quite normally around equally normal people.

Using the six-step problem-solving procedure, the Siegals define Harley's problem as "pooping and peeing in the house anytime, anywhere." Can they refine their definition by finding out why?

"When you gotta go, you gotta go!" says Bruce.

True, but does Harley do it in the presence of other dogs? Does he prefer one or two particular places?

"Nope," replies Bruce confidently. "Anytime, anywhere, doesn't matter who or what's around."

"We love Harley," Jolene adds, "but he's ruining our rugs. We can't put up with this much longer."

Jolene's statement tells us that the Siegals want to change the behavior; they are unwilling to ignore it or accept it, but they don't want to get rid of the pup, either. The solution? Properly housebreak Harley. But how?

"Even though his messes bother me, hitting the dog bothers me more," admits Bruce.

Jolene agrees. "Although a lot of people recommend sticking his nose in it, that bothers *me* too. Isn't there a more natural way to toilet train a pup?"

The Siegals decide to collect some information. From a local trainer and Harley's vet they learn four very important facts about dogs and their waste products:

- The canine gastrocolic reflex causes dogs to defecate and urinate after eating and drinking. Food or water entering the dog's digestive system stimulates stool and urine production.
- The bitch normally cleans up the stool and urine of nursing pups. The pup learns that its mother expects such "gifts."
- Most dogs won't mess where they eat or sleep.
- Scent attracts dogs to relieve themselves in certain areas.

Fortunately, owners can use a housebreaking method that takes advantage of all four of these behavioral facts.

The Siegals put Harley on a strict schedule of both food and water intake, cautioning Beth that between-meal snacks interfere with Harley's housebreaking. Because they know it's natural for the mother to stimulate the pups to urinate and defecate after nursing and to keep them clean, the Siegals realize Harley shouldn't see *them* cleaning up his messes.

"I always thought making Harley watch the cleanup would teach him how naughty he was, how much work he was making for us," Jolene confesses. "Now I realize we were just replacing his mother in his eyes. Allowing him to see us clean up just reassured him he'd done the *right* thing! Gee, pups can have such a short memory! Just like little kids. If we don't catch Harley in the act, yelling at him after the fact only confuses him. Now when it happens, one of us takes him outside, while someone else cleans up. It's not easy. Sometimes I want to yell at him or swat him, but now I see that only delivers the wrong message."

In addition to making these changes, the Siegals thoroughly clean any areas Harley soils so the lingering scent won't attract him. When they observe how Harley sniffs around before he urinates or defecates, they realize he *does* prefer specific areas for relieving himself. Although they first thought he scattered his messes randomly, they soon realize the pup never messes in any bedrooms or in the kitchen corner where the family keeps his food and water bowls.

Should the parents let Harley sleep with them at night or confine him to a very small corner of the kitchen? Even though some owners worry about restricting an unhousebroken dog to the bedroom at night, few dogs will soil their master's sleeping quarters any more than they will their own. Some owners leash the dog to the leg of the bed to further limit its area, or place the dog's bed on the floor beside their own; others prefer denning.

The Denning Dilemma

What is denning? In this era of quick-fix solutions denning is perhaps the quickest, most lasting training technique an owner can use. Denning means confining the dog in a crate big enough for it, with a blanket and a favorite toy. Many animal lovers automatically cringe at the very idea. "Put Harley in *prison*?" Jolene cries defensively. "Dogs want to be free, just like people." Sure they do; the desire to be free is a strong instinct in dogs. But although dogs desire freedom to investigate stimuli at will, they also yearn to feel safe. When Bruce convinced Jolene to put Harley in a fiberglass kennel whenever they're gone, they remove the dog's ability, and therefore his instinctive need to protect the area. He no longer *has* to protect that big house and yard, and feels safe from all those frightening sights, scents, and sounds as he sleeps contentedly in his little den.

If denning strikes you as unreasonable or cruel, try putting yourself in the dog's place. Pretend you're a young, inexperienced 10-pound pup left in charge of an entire household. You hear more than four times what any human hears, your vision is ten times more sensitive to any motion, and your sense of smell detects odors that escape most people. What's that noise? What moved over there? Is that a good or bad smell? Because you lack sufficient experience, you perceive all these stimuli as threatening, and unless you can investigate them, you must live in constant fear. If I were in that position, I'd crawl under the nearest bed or couch and create my own den, which is exactly what many dogs do.

What message does denning communicate to the inexperienced pup or timid adult dog? "I understand how being alone and protecting this place frightens you, so I want to relieve that pressure." Owners who view denning as a violation of the dog's freedom once again project human values on their dogs. Although the instinct to be free is strong, most confident dogs are quite contented when alone in a restricted environment.

What about confining Harley to a small corner of the kitchen at night? Although this may take advantage of his natural instinct not to soil where he eats, it also isolates the pup from the rest of the family; dogs are social animals who like to be with other dogs or people.

If the owner finds having the dog in the bedroom unacceptable, denning offers a more effective alternative because it provides a more limited and secure area for the dog. Even if the pup is unrestrained in the bedroom at night, it will respond favorably to denning when it must be left alone in the house.

Using Normal and Natural Tendencies

Because one or another Siegal is home most of the time, they're able to schedule trips outdoors for Harley to relieve himself. Realizing the importance of timing and consistency, they build his schedule around their *normal* pattern, thereby avoiding a major setback many of us encounter: inconsistency leading to a confused (an unhousebroken) dog. Because we want the housebreaking accomplished as quickly as possible and any mess and smell out of the house, we're often willing to change our life-style completely to accomplish the task. Every time the pup looks at us, we rush it outdoors. Then once it hasn't messed in the house for a week or two, we assume it's housebroken and resume our regular routine. Suddenly, instead of being let out twelve times a day, the pup finds itself outdoors only after its feedings and at bedtime. Not surprisingly, the pup housebroken under the old routine becomes unhousebroken when the owners return to the normal schedule.

Just as they noticed Harley has special places where he *wouldn't* go in the house, the Siegals recognize the pup also prefers certain spots in the yard, so they select one of his special places in a far corner away from Beth's play area. After every meal, first thing in the morning and last thing at night, they take the pup to his corner and lavishly praise him when he relieves himself. Why not let Harley go where he wants? Because dogs use urine and stool to mark their territory; the more they spread it around, the bigger their territory and the more protective they must be. If Harley lays claim to the neighbor's flower garden, the Siegals will have a hard time keeping him from spoiling prize roses and turning good neighbors into enemies. And because Beth invites friends to play in the yard and her parents enjoy outdoor entertaining in the summer, limiting Harley's area limits his protective (and instinctively, sometimes aggressive) instincts to a small area, and permits the family to enjoy the yard.

By keeping Harley on a strict feeding and watering schedule, confining him when the family can't keep an eye on him, thoroughly cleaning any soiled areas in the house, and taking him to his own special area to relieve himself regularly, the Siegals effectively housebreak Harley in a month.

What about paper training? Of course, we've all heard advice from experienced owners about paper training, because it does work. But using this method creates two unnecessary problems. Given the dog's lack of detail vision, it may easily confuse your daily newspaper with his toilet. Second, if you want your dog to eventually go outside, you wind up training the dog twice—once to papers, and again to the outdoors.

Territorial Marking: The Nose Knows

Harley remained totally housebroken until the Wednesday before his fourth birthday, when the Siegals come home to find a large wet spot on the family room rug.

"Maybe he drank too much water and couldn't hold it," says Beth.

Bruce and Jolene agree, but when it happens the next day, and the day after that, they begin to worry.

"Let's take him to the vet's, Bruce," Jolene insists. "Maybe he has a bladder infection."

After the vet gives Harley a complete physical examination, she says he's perfectly normal. "Harley wouldn't mess in one place if he had an infection. Dogs with infections either try to hold their urine because it hurts to go, or they leave little puddles everywhere. If they can't hold it, they might mess during the night or if no one's home, but not usually in the same place."

So *why* is he messing in the house? The vet suggests that Harley is marking his territory. But why does he do it in the family room? Why now? The vet tells them dogs often begin marking in the house if a strange dog threatens them or other dogs urinate inside. Beth reminds her parents that her uncle had stopped by to show them his new pup about the same time Harley started peeing on the rug.

"But your Uncle Brian's pup's a chicken," Bruce remarks. "Surely, she wouldn't scare Harley?"

She didn't. Harley scared her—in fact, scared the pee right out of her, right on the family room rug! In response to the pup's normal submissive urination in the presence of a more dominant dog, Harley adds his own calling card to the other dog's.

Using the same white vinegar and water solution she used when Harley was a pup, Jolene thoroughly cleans the area where her brother's pup went. When no one is home to distract Harley from going near the area, the

Siegals keep the door to the family room tightly closed. Although they can't detect any odor after cleaning the rug, they realize Harley's sense of smell is much more sensitive than theirs and that he's become conditioned to urinating in response to the scent of the pup's urine in the rug. Because the odor triggers Harley's marking behavior, once they remove the smell they eliminate the original reason for the behavior although it may take a while for Harley to forget completely.

Because Harley is an older male dog and strongly attached to the Siegals and their property, it takes longer to discourage the marking than it did to housebreak him. However, the family observes enough improvement by the end of the first month to encourage them to maintain the changes for another thirty days.

Glands Away!

Would you be surprised to learn that among the ingredients that make expensive perfume expensive are substances secreted from highly specialized anal glands in civets and musk deer? These animals normally use such secretions, containing specialized hormones that stimulate the sense of smell, to mark their territories and attract mates.

Dogs, too, possess such glands. They are located within the rectum and function much as they do in wild animals. They aid territorial marking and attract mates. But two characteristics of the modern dog's life thwart their normal functions: we frequently spay or castrate our pets, and we strongly discourage the formation of dog packs in our society. The former maker attracting a mate pointless, the latter limits territoriality. So our dogs possess secreting glands but no socially acceptable means to express them.

If your dog either doesn't secrete enough to bother you or can sufficiently empty its glands via the pressure of stool against the sacs during defecation, you probably never think about anal glands, and might not even know they exist. On the other hand, if your dog secretes voluminously and/or empties its glands frequently, or can't empty them, you probably think about them a lot.

The voluminous secretor provides its owner with a memorable olfactory experience. The odor of anal glands lasts, and lasts. And lasts. Normally the substance is a milky-white fluid which the dog sprays when excited or frightened. As Dufie taught me, trying to clean a semi-transparent spray off white walls takes more than strong soap and elbow grease; and like perfume, even a drop can permeate a room.

If your dog only displays this behavior in the presence of other dogs, particularly those of the opposite sex, neutering (spaying or castrating) may solve the problem. If your pup behaves like Harley Siegal, it lacks confidence; sudden loud noises or other events that startle an inexperienced pup may lead it to involuntarily empty its glands. As the pup matures and experiences more and your consistent confidence-building training takes hold, such incidents cease to produce this fear response. However, if we frighten pups during what they consider normal activity (as when Bruce went after Harley while the pup was defecating), it may require special effort to restore their confidence.

Although the animal who liberally expresses its anal glands repels us and our visiting relatives, the dog who can't express them can pose a serious medical problem. Whether a result of life-style, reproductive status, or some anatomical abnormality, some dogs can't or won't empty full glands. In such cases, the dogs initially experience discomfort which they try to relieve by dragging their rear ends across the ground or floor. How many times have you witnessed such behavior and imagined worms? If a dog drags itself because it has worms, however, you should *see* worms, usually short flat tapeworm segments or spaghettilike roundworms. In the majority of cases, rump-dragging behavior stems from the pressure or irritation of impacted anal glands. If the animal can't relieve the pressure, the glands may become infected and abscess. When this happens, the area becomes enlarged and super-sensitive, the animal grows restless, laps the area constantly, and may even spike a fever and stop eating. When the abscess opens, pus, some blood, and anal gland secretion flow freely onto the rug, the bedspread, or wherever the dog happens to be.

Although anal gland infections generally respond well to treatment, they can become chronic and require surgery to remove the glands and surrounding tissue. Wise owners find it's much easier to have the glands emptied when the dog begins to show signs of discomfort. Veterinarians usually empty the glands in one of two ways. Some apply firm upward pressure over the glands externally, milking the contents out the anus. Others prefer to exert pressure simultaneously on the inside and outside of the full gland with a gloved hand; this method also enables the vet to palpate the rectal area for any abnormalities. Obviously, it's not recommended that owners use the intrarectal approach. However, some owners of dogs with recurring anal gland problems do prefer to use the external method at home. Discuss this with your vet before you try it. Remember, dogs don't like to be restrained; and restraining a dog to crank its tail over its back and squeeze its anus isn't something it will passively accept. Your vet can tell you whether it's necessary to express your dog's anal glands, whether your dog has the personality to allow this without you or it being hurt, and how to do it correctly.

The Social Sniffer

Have you ever been embarrassed by an otherwise well-mannered dog burying its nose in your crotch or goosing you from behind at a bridge party? Such social sniffing can occur in all breeds, but seems more common in scent hounds such as beagles, bassets, and bloodhounds, to name a few. We call such breeds scent hounds because people originally bred them to hunt game by tracking its scent. Like many sporting breeds, most of these animals are now family pets rather than hunting dogs, but they've retained their keen sense of smell.

Social sniffing causes problems because dogs automatically nuzzle moist areas where odors are the most pungent. Consequently, they hone in on the same human anatomical areas—the mouth and crotch—that attract them to other dogs, the very areas most humans find most sacred and private.

So how do you apologize to Ms. Wonderful who finally agrees to join your bridge club when, the instant she sits down, your St. Bernard plops his head in her lap and makes disgusting snuffling noises? Not only will he probably continue making these bothersome sounds, he may also display the flahmen reaction, a highly specific olfactory-based response to certain odors. Dogs and many other animals have a small bump just behind their middle-upper incisors (the small teeth between the fangs), a remnant of a highly sophisticated olfactory system. When animals perceive a particularly enticing odor they wish to explore more thoroughly, they pull the upper lip back and open the mouth slightly to expose this receptor; some animals also close their eyes slightly. Now Ms. Wonderful not only has to deal with the snuffling and some drool on her new silk skirt, she must also contend with what appears to be a hypnotized dog with a stupid expression on its face. And because the majority of these enticing odors are hormonal in origin, it's also highly likely the dog will also experience an erection. Hello disgust, good-bye Ms. Wonderful.

Although crotch sniffing, the flahmen reaction, and erections are normal canine responses to scents from other animals, few humans appreciate this form of communication, partly because people misinterpret what a dog's sniffing says about them ("I'm dirty." "I stink." "I smell like a dog.") In any case, sniffing problems seldom evoke *unemotional* responses from their victims.

Under these circumstances, I suggest you say something like, "Why don't we go *out* for a drink?" to Ms. Wonderful and name the poshest club in town, leaving the dog to evaluate his scent data in private. Or else lock him in your bedroom for the evening.

On a more long-term basis, however, social sniffers are best handled with setups. First train the dog to orient to a word or sound. Once you achieve a good orienting response, invite a friend over, and as soon as the dog exhibits any type of unacceptable sniffing, orient it and distract it with a favorite toy or simple command. ("Harley, get your ball.") Lavishly praise this preferred behavior. Some owners find it easier to train the dog to leave all visitors alone; others allow the dog restricted shoe or pantleg sniffing. Whichever you prefer, critically define acceptable behavior and then consistently orient and distract the dog anytime it exceeds those limits. Inviting friends over *specifically* for such a purpose helps eliminate the embarrassment and inconsistency that so often interfere when training occurs in the presence of unsuspecting guests.

Good Smell, Bad Smell

Do owners and dogs *ever* agree about odors? I'm not sure. Like all the senses, smell is highly subjective; one person's garlic is another's rose. However, I do think most owners intuitively recognize the smell of a healthy dog. Owners who have forged a strong bond with their dogs recognize and take comfort in their pets' unique blends of odors. They can often sniff out ear infections before discharge appears, sense when their female is coming into heat by the faintly different smell of her urine, or detect digestive or dental problems when mouth odors change slightly.

Similarly, dogs zero in on beloved owners' perfume or after-shave, even picking up the scent in crowded rooms or the middle of the woods. One dedicated Italian greyhound loved his mistress so much, he literally fainted every time she said good-bye. It turned out he was allergic to her new perfume. When she bent down to give him a farewell hug, he got a big whiff of it and couldn't breathe. By the time the distraught woman's husband got the poor dog to the vet's, he had already recovered. Thank goodness the woman didn't accompany the dog to the vet's or he might have died.

Just as we tend to lump the majority of the dog's

natural odors into the category of "Wow, what stinks!," we also hold our own peculiar notions about what smells good *to* our dogs. Invariably, we define what smells good to a dog in terms of what *tastes* good to *us*. In the next chapter, we'll see how this tendency can create not only headaches for us, but stomachaches for our dogs.

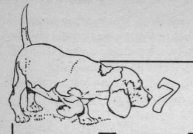

7

Taste: The Cable from the Table

Sheila Albrecht felt so lonely after her youngest child married and left home, she bought Pandora, a blue merle collie, to keep her company. Although the breeder recommended Sheila feed the pup a balanced dry food, Sheila began adding table scraps to Pandora's food by the end of their first week together.

"I'm so used to cooking for more than one, I always make too much. I can't bear to throw food away. Besides, Pandora *loves* to eat what I eat."

Sheila shares all her food with the pup, rewards her with treats when she obeys simple commands, and frequently bestows treats and tidbits just to win Pandora's excited response. The relationship was mutually rewarding until Sheila's children and grandchildren came home to celebrate Thanksgiving. Pandora begged constantly and even stole food from the children. If they tried to ignore her, she barked and pestered them until they gave her what she wanted.

"Lord, Mom, if that were my dog, I'd shoot it!" shouted her son in exasperation after the pup upset a tray of cheese and crackers, scattering it all over the dining room floor.

After her family left, Sheila absently fed her dog bits of leftover turkey as she cleared the table; then she gave the pup the usual doggy treat after Pandora relieved herself outdoors. Hours later, with Pandora settled contentedly beside her on the couch, Sheila still couldn't forget her son's angry words. Was there something wrong with him, or did he have a point? Does Pandora's normal behavior appear abnormal to others?

A Matter of Good Taste

Many people believe their tastes in food reflect their personal philosophy and life-style. For example, consider these statements:

"Just give me a pizza and a six-pack of beer."

"The squid at Chez Charles was superb, but the watercress soup needed more oregano."

If you're like most people, you easily assign distinct personalities and even different educational and socio-economic backgrounds to different people's eating habits. After all, doesn't the latter statement reflect refined breeding and good taste? We somehow assume that the Boston Brahmin, Harvard-educated investment broker dines on haute cuisine, whereas our unkempt clod of a cousin loves beer and pizza.

People routinely form food associations unrelated to

the food's natural qualities—protein, fat, and carbohydrate—or their ability to digest it. Don't teenage girls who select diets primarily to achieve clear complexions and trim figures express their desire for happiness and success through their eating habits? Aren't the fraternity brothers wolfing burgers and chugging beer expressing their need for power and virility? "C'mon, bet you can't eat all of that!" Those who fear ill-health or aging often define food as a protective barrier: "An apple a day keeps the doctor away." "Eat wise, stay young!" Every day we learn that some previously acceptable food might cause cancer in rats, and those who fear cancer shun that food. On the other hand, magazine articles tout some new diet as a cure for colds, sexual malaise, or acne, and those of us afflicted with such problems eagerly adopt it. Many religions use bread and wine in their most holy sacraments; and all of us celebrate special occasions with lavish feasts. Our whole society seems to revolve around food and its many meanings. No wonder dog owners find it difficult to feed their dogs dry kibble!

Because "one man's meat is another man's poison," we mistakenly assume the same holds true for dogs. Don't our big, brawny bulldogs deserve lean, red meat, and shouldn't our delicate, refined poodles crave chocolate-covered truffles? Before we examine the problems caused by such attitudes, let's review the role taste plays in the wild dog's life. Remember that taste is just one of the many functions performed by the canine tongue. Although the dog does have anatomical structures similar to taste buds in the human tongue, it's impossible to say whether dogs experience the sweet, sour, salty, or bitter sensations we do. In fact, because there's no way we can be sure that *my* salty is the same as *your* salty, we'll never be able to define salty for a dog.

Actually, dogs use their sense of taste much differently than we do. Although no one can say for sure why the dog's sense of taste developed the way it did, we can assume it primarily benefited the species' survival rather than its casual social interaction. Taste determined whether or not a given food might be harmful or beneficial, and any animal unable to differentiate harmful from beneficial food grew weak, ill, and possibly died. Similarly, those who learned to identify safe and beneficial food grew stronger and healthier, increasing their chances to survive and reproduce. As a tool for survival, taste helped the animal evaluate its food in terms of quality (beneficial or dangerous) and quantity (too much, just enough, too little). Little, if any, emotion accompanied such measurement.

The Emotional Lunchbox

So how did Pandora progress from a straightforward, biological feeder—one eating to fill her physiological needs—to one apparently attaching strong emotions to her food? When we humans decided to domesticate animals, we first made them dependent on us for something vital, something absolutely necessary to their survival. In other words, by providing a dog with food and preventing it from hunting its own, we made it our slave; we oriented it, and held it to us, with food. Primitive people selectively bred certain animals whose characteristics fit their needs, gradually weaning those animals from the skills required for survival in the wild. Although they bred some dogs to be hunters, they didn't permit them to eat their catch. Similarly, dogs bred and trained to herd weren't allowed to turn their charges into convenient meals. In order to insure this acceptable behavior, people provided ample alternative food for their dogs.

Eventually, a bond formed between people and dogs. As the dogs became integrated into the human pack, people began sharing more of their lives with them, sometimes going so far as to treat them almost as members of their own species. The dog shared the leftovers of a harvest feast and reaped its share of rewards after a successful day's hunt. It didn't take long for talented canine mimics to adopt some of the intricate symbolism humans attach to food.

Until about ten years ago, owners could justify feeding dogs "people" food because few commercial dog foods offered balanced diets. Now, however, the prevalence of nutritionally balanced commercial products negates the old justification. Still, people constantly slip their pets tidbits they themselves find tasty. Why does an intelligent, sensitive pet owner like Sheila Albrecht unnecessarily ply her pup with her own favorite foods? Why does she bribe or reward Pandora with sweets? Is it because she loves her dog? Does food equal love? To some extent yes, but Sheila also lacks confidence in her ability to train Pandora and keep the pup's love *without* food. Like primitive people hoping to maintain a wild dog's allegiance by providing it with an abundant supply of food, we often use our turkey and cheese, yummies and chewies to accomplish the same ends.

A similar lack of confidence in themselves and their dogs' *desire* to respond to them leads many owners to use food to orient their pets, waving biscuits or other treats every time they want the dog's attention. Unfortunately, this tactic will inevitably lead to a situation where the dog pays attention not to its owner's commands, but to the biscuits alone.

Orienting with food is like sending a postcard with a five-dollar bill taped to it. It's excessive, unnecessary, and does little to ensure the message reaches its destination intact.

Slamming the Lid on Pandora's Lunchbox

Unless a dog's food associations and feeding habits result in obesity or other medical problems, most owners tend to treat their taste communication with their dogs rather casually. Like Sheila, they fall into a comfortable pattern until someone says something like:

"You actually cook steak for your dog?"

"You let a dog eat off your plate?"

"How can you stand that constant begging?"

"I'm sorry, we can't board your dog again. She's such a fussy eater."

In the face of such wounding comments, many owners vacillate between accepting the feeding pattern and feeling good about it, and changing the pattern and/or their feelings. Until Thanksgiving, Sheila thoroughly enjoyed Pandora's reaction to food, never considering it a problem at all. However, her son's angry words upset her, and she began to feel insecure. Because the six-step problem-solving approach makes it easier to understand a conflicting point of view, Sheila decides to use it to define the problem and possible solutions in terms of her son's as well as her own viewpoint.

In Sheila's case, step one poses no great hurdle because she *does* believe her relationship with Pandora is normal. Because she doesn't think there's a problem, she defines it in terms of her son's point of view:

Problem	When the Problem Occurs/Occurred	Possible Explanations
Pandora reacts too strongly to food.	All the time, but especially when company visits.	It's normal puppy behavior.
		I've spoiled her.
		Company excites her.
		She's afraid she won't get enough to eat.
		She had some bad experience before I got her.
		Something is lacking in her dog food.

Sheila is surprised she can come up with so many reasons for a heretofore nonexistent problem.

Because she plans to have Pandora spayed in a few months, Sheila visits the vet to discuss the surgery and the dog's eating habits. The vet assures her Pandora is healthy and getting the correct amount and kind of dog food; but he cautions against the extra tidbits.

"When Pandora reaches adulthood, her nutritional needs will be much less than now. Furthermore, spayed females tend to require fewer calories to stay healthy and maintain a reasonable weight. If you continue slipping her table food, she could get very fat after her surgery."

Sheila takes such pride in her own trim figure she hates the thought of slender Pandora getting fat, so she resolves to scrutinize her own taste and food-related beliefs.

Where do we seek information when we suspect *we're* the problem? Although I've known owners so entangled in emotional food relationships with their pets that psychological counseling seemed warranted, most owners can work it out themselves, especially if they have a few honest friends. For example, rather than agonizing over whether her beliefs about food are good or bad, Sheila merely accepts them and concentrates on their effect on Pandora:

- Pandora is constantly looking for food.
- Sheila's children and grandchildren think the dog behaves badly.
- Sheila reacts negatively to her family because of their reaction to her dog.
- Sheila reacts negatively to Pandora because of the tension the dog creates between her and her family.
- Pandora could get fat and develop health problems because of her diet.
- Sheila's confidence in herself as a good dog owner has taken a beating.

When Sheila recognizes the wide range of effects her well-intentioned feeding patterns have created, she decides to change not only the pattern, but her own attitudes. She lists different ways she could stop Pandora's attachment to people food and treats in favor of her balanced dry dog food:

Problem	*Possible Solutions*
Pandora reacts too strongly to food because of the extra tidbits she gets.	—Gradually decrease the amount of people food and treats.
	—Feed her nothing but dog food.
	—Switch Pandora to a more palatable dog food such as semimoist burgers or canned food.
	—Substitute some other expression of love for the extra food.

As she scans the list, Sheila remembers the vet's approval of Pandora's current dog food. But if it's so good, why doesn't Pandora like it? Sheila calls the breeder for a second opinion.

"Ms. Albrecht, that's one of the best dog foods on the market. I feed it to all my dogs."

"But Pandora hates it! I have to add cheese and meat and dog treats to get her to eat it."

The breeder politely suggests Sheila's supplementation has actually taught Pandora to disregard the plain food.

"Even a healthy pup routinely skips a meal now and then, but an unknowledgeable owner often thinks it's sick or dislikes the food. To find out, they offer roast beef and slosh gravy on the dog food. If the pup then eats the food, it does so for reasons other than biological needs; its natural system had told it *not* to eat that day.

The pup also learns it can make its owner change its food simply by ignoring what's offered."

Sheila shakes her head. "I assumed dogs preferred gravy and roast beef because they *taste* better."

What's the real message Sheila communicates when she says this? The real message is "I assumed dogs prefer gravy and roast beef because they taste better *to me*." At the core of Sheila's definition of good taste lies her belief that eating and offering these foods is "better." If she wants to·treat, that is, show love to, herself or those around her, she serves delightful foods. Realizing this, Sheila quickly concludes that roast beef and other treats mean more than just "food" to her, and that she's communicating that message to Pandora. To Sheila, Pandora's dog food *is* "just food"; but all that people food comes loaded with love and companionship for *both* dog and owner.

When Sheila offers Pandora extra food, she exhibits an attitude and body language entirely different from those she displays when she fills the dog's bowl with kibble. As she saves that last bit of cheese for her dog, Sheila imagines how pleased Pandora will be with the treat, and she eventually offers it with loving words and gestures. On the receiving end of communication, Pandora first responds enthusiastically to her owner's display of affection, *then* she eats the cheese. Note the subtlety here. Like people, dogs are social animals craving the company of others. Although Pandora actually prefers Sheila's company to cheese, the pup connects the cheese to Sheila's love, especially when her mistress lavishly rewards her for wolfing it down. Left alone with 10 pounds of cheese free from emotional associations, Pandora might eat greedily at first, anticipating the accompanying human companionship; but when none arrives, she obeys her natural physiological impulses, eating only to satisfy her appetite, then quitting. On the other hand, Sheila could have fed her dog a ton of cheese piece by piece, reward by reward. When Pandora upset the cheese tray at Thanksgiving, she was simply shouting at the family for the love and attention she had come to expect.

How can Sheila change an animal whose behavior signals love? It isn't easy. Adding her self-evaluation to the information gathered from the veterinarian and breeder, Sheila decides to feed Pandora the same dog food and find some way besides treat-feeding to communicate her love.

Unfortunately, Pandora has constructed a food-love association every bit as strong as Sheila's, so when her owner withholds snacks, the collie feels Sheila's love has subsided, too. Although initially Sheila thought her resolve strong enough to support a "No snacks, period!" stance, after two days she suffers guilt and frustration. Pandora's whining, doleful stares at the refrigerator, and constant nuzzling while Sheila tries to eat leave both owner and dog emotionally drained.

On the third day, Sheila decides to put Pandora out on her run while she prepares and eats her own meals. Only after she's thrown away or stored the leftovers and washed and put away all dishes, does she permit the dog back into the house. When Pandora bounds inside, Sheila devotes her full attention to her. After Sheila's breakfast and dinner, she sets aside time for training sessions during which she teaches the pup to respond to simple commands, using sound orientation and eye contact and heaping lavish praise instead of food for rewards. In a short time, Pandora looks forward to her run during Sheila's mealtimes because she knows it precedes their love-sharing sessions. Pandora's ball can signal love as well as food.

By relying on companionship and love in the form of teaching and sharing, Sheila not only eliminates Pandora's negative behavior around food, but she gains a well-trained, healthier pet. When her family arrives for Christmas dinner, they can't believe the change.

"Mom, did you get a new dog?" her dumbfounded son jokes as Pandora sits quietly during the meal.

Sheila beams proudly and scratches Pandora's ear. "Yes, I do have a new dog—and she has a brand new owner. Isn't it wonderful?"

The Senior Gourmet

Pandora developed into a well-mannered pet, but food problems arose again almost ten years later when her decreased digestive ability began to limit how much and what she could eat. At first the aging dog occasionally threw up and passed a lot of gas after a large, regular meal; then she began to eat less and increase the interval between feedings. Because Sheila associates a healthy appetite with good health, when her older pet begins skipping meals, she worries. Recalling the food-related problems she experienced when Pandora was young, she decides to define the problem before she relapses into the old feelings of frustration and guilt:

Problem	When Problem Occurs/ Occurred	Possible Explanations
Pandora doesn't eat regularly anymore.	Every 2 to 3 days she skips a meal.	She's ill. Something's wrong with the food. She doesn't need as much food.

When Sheila takes Pandora to the vet, she learns that older dogs often have difficulty digesting the crude fiber (carbohydrate) and the form of protein found in some commercial dog foods.

"Gas, which may cause Pandora some discomfort, is just an end product of incomplete digestion. Like Pavlov's dogs, she soon connected eating with that discomfort and curtailed her food intake accordingly. Don't worry that she now prefers to snack on her dog food rather than eat one or two larger meals. Let her skip meals. Let her natural system regulate her feeding."

Sheila takes some comfort from the vet's statement that normal aging changes can decrease a dog's calorie requirements as much as 75 percent. However, a thorough examination does reveal genuine digestive problems. The vet suggests a low fat, low fiber, quality protein canned food especially designed for older dogs.

"However, be careful to avoid the food-love trap. If you hover over Pandora while she eats or offer the food with some emotional overtones, she'll be aware of it. In spite of your concern for her health, make any dietary changes *unemotionally*. Need I remind you to avoid giving her any table food? Lots of owners try to tempt dogs with digestive problems to eat by offering something like milk, which they find soothing during their own digestive upsets. That not only establishes the food-love cycle, it can cause diarrhea and make the dog even more uncomfortable."

Sheila immediately implements the recommended dietary changes and, although she carefully tracks the amount Pandora eats, she doesn't bother the dog while she's eating. By the end of two weeks, Pandora seems like a new dog again.

The Chicken Soup Trap

Almost all of us cherish fond memories or fantasies of a loved one administering chicken soup to pull us through some illness. Most cultures believe eating certain foods can cure all sorts of physical, mental, and emotional ailments. Consequently, when our dogs get sick, we invariably gauge their willingness to eat as a measure of their degree of illness. Let's consider a typical sick dog to see what problems can arise.

When Peaches, the Majewskis' five-year-old Pomeranian, came down with an intestinal virus, the little creature vomited and had diarrhea for several days before the owners took her to the animal hospital where she received intravenous fluids and medication. The dog barely survived the ordeal, and when the owners finally brought her home, they received instructions to feed their pet a bland diet of rice and chicken for several days, then gradually wean her off it. However, as Peaches slowly recovered, rather than putting her back on dog food, the

Majewskis kept feeding the bland diet recommended by the vet; but they also started adding other meats, vegetables, and seasonings, as well as numerous cookies and treats.

"I'm becoming a great canine chef," remarked Mrs. Majewski, spooning a handful of liver on Peaches' pile of chicken and rice. "Now she's so healthy, she eats like a horse. I don't want her ever to get sick again!"

Six months later the Majewskis take Peaches back to the vet, but this time to try to reverse the effects of her high-caloried and unbalanced diet which has begun to take its toll. The dog's coat is dull and dry, she's plagued by almost constant diarrhea and gas, and she's so fat, her owners worry about the strain on her heart and skeletal system.

Basically, the Majewskis must repeat Sheila Albrecht's self-evaluation. In this case, however, the family has adopted an emotional association with food as a result of some very dramatic circumstances. They suffered some harrowing days trying to get Peaches to eat when she first became ill. Not only wouldn't she eat, she became sicker and sicker, and the family soon grew to believe that "When Peaches doesn't eat, she gets sicker." Then they endured those agonizing hospital days when the dog's survival seemed doubtful, followed by her painfully slow recovery. For ten days, life seemed to hinge on whether or not the Pomeranian ate. What a joyful day when the vet announced the dog had eaten her first bite of food and would recover! So great was their relief that the family later encouraged their pet to eat and eat and eat.

Whereas Sheila equated food with love and companionship, the Majewskis equate it with good health. Because Peaches' illness frightened them so badly, they felt they must take extreme precautions not to let it happen again; so they shunned her former diet even though the dog had eaten it her entire life, and had been perfectly healthy before the viral attack.

"If Peaches survives, she's going to have the best of everything," Mrs. Majewski vowed when Peaches lay comatose. Little did she know her deep love for her pet would make the dog sick again.

Can the six-step problem-solving process help now? After defining the problem, Mrs. Majewski lists all the foods Peaches has been eating: chicken, rice, peas, corn, tomatoes, beef, pork, carrots, potatoes, bread, eggs, milk, cookies, potato chips, ice cream, turkey, candy, and popcorn.

"Lord, look at this list!" she exclaims. "It's got all *our* favorite foods on it!"

The vet compares the list with Peaches' nutritional requirements and shows the owners how their home-made diet gives their dog too many calories and not enough vital nutrients.

"Can't I add vitamin supplements?" Mrs. Majewski wants to know.

Although that's possible, it won't solve all the nutritional deficiencies, so the vet suggests they simply put Peaches back on her old diet. "Can I be blunt?" the vet asks. "Peaches doesn't have a dog problem at all. She has a *people* problem."

This so shocks the Majewskis they ask the vet to hospitalize their pet until she's eating dog food again. That will give them time to deal with their own feelings and break the habit of cooking especially for the dog. Like so many owners, the Majewskis gradually realize their own deep-seated beliefs about food will take concentration to change.

The answer? Obviously, the Majewskis must learn to feel good about feeding their dog a nutritional diet. However, fear can overwhelm even the most convincing advice. Fear erodes confidence, lack of confidence destroys consistency, and inconsistency breeds failure, which of course leads us back to the beginning of the cycle. Until the Majewskis resolve their fears, Peaches will continue to languish at the mercy of the food = love equation.

A Smorgasbord of Miscommunication

Before ending our discussion of taste, let's examine a few examples of other taste-based miscommunication. What about owners who supplement the dog's diet with lean red meat, vitamins, and minerals? Unless the animal is on *specific* supplementation recommended to solve a *specific* nutritional deficit, such embellishments fall into the category of miscommunication: "I take vitamins because they keep me healthy, so I give them to Suzette too"; "Because wild dogs eat raw meat, my Siberian needs it too." Such notions force food-related prejudices onto our dogs. Rather than being emotionally based like Sheila's, these project some incorrect assumptions about our dog's nutritional needs. If owners who supplement vitamins, raw eggs, and meat, take the time to collect information, they may learn some startling facts.

For example, let's examine the lean red meat phenomenon. If you read ads for dog food or watch dog food commercials, you soon realize that references to red meat sell dog food. (Actually, dog food marketing now seems to be separated into two distinct groups: those who believe consumers prefer to think of their dogs as displaced meat-eating wild creatures, and those who feel owners like a strong people-food component—cheese and gravy, for example—in their pet's daily fare.) If you envision your dog as needing meat "like wild dogs," chances are you envision it eating a bowl of USDA ground meat or beef. Let's compare that with the actual wild dog fare. In the wild, predators consume all or parts of the entire animal; unlike humans, they haven't developed a preference for merely the large, lean muscle masses. And because most predators prey on plant-eating herbivores, their diet also includes vegetation-stuffed intestines, something not found in USDA meat. What does this mean for the all-meat diet? It's an unbalanced diet.

Another point to consider is that meat, as a source of protein, is a most difficult substance to digest, requiring maximum digestive ability. Although most young animals have that ability, many lose it with normal aging changes. The result can be a dog experiencing periodic digestive distress that may lead to permanent damage.

As for supplementation, although it may not produce the obesity that often results from food equals love miscommunication, it can result in problems such as diarrhea, gas, skeletal and growth problems in pups, and more. Supplementing owners assume the dog's system will use only what it needs and get rid of the excess with no wear and tear on the system. It doesn't work that way. Whatever enters the dog's mouth must be handled one way or another with corresponding stress on the entire body, *whether the dog derives any benefit from the supplement or not.* If you're not sure whether your feeding practices are sound, state them in the form of a problem: "I think I might be oversupplementing Georgio's diet when I add bone meal to it," and work it through the six-step process. If you discover in the course of collecting information that his diet *is* deficient in calcium and phosphorus and the amount and form of supplementation is correct, then you know you're responding to *his* needs. On the other hand, if your information tells you Georgio's diet is sufficient without the bone meal, you'll feel more confident about discontinuing the supplementation regardless what anyone else says.

What do dogs who eat things we find disgusting communicate? If we accept the fact we can't know what tastes good to our dogs, we must also realize we can't judge what's bad, either. Although it shocked the Majewskis to learn Peaches' diet composed of their favorite foods hurt the Pomeranian's health, it horrified them when the vet said that Peaches' munching rabbit "raisins" was normal. Normal? In their minds, nothing could be more harmful or abnormal than eating stool.

Here again, the six-step process can help us understand the dog's point of view. By stating such behavior as a problem ("Peaches eats rabbit droppings." "Sydney eats dead squirrels." "Edgar eats his own stool.") we can systematically define and resolve it. If it really bothers them, Peaches' and Sydney's owners might solve the problem by confining their pets. If it doesn't, they might alter their feelings about it. On the other hand, Edgar's owners could discover their dog has medical problems such as a decrease in the enzymes necessary to digest his current diet. In such cases the dog's ability to digest food may be so poor, its stool is more like food than waste and therefore worthy of (re)consumption. In these cases, sometimes just changing the diet solves the problem. Other times, a complete medical work-up and possible long-term medication is required.

Sometimes, the way we orient our dogs toward food combines with the other senses to create even more dilemmas. When the Overmeyers feed Verushka, their

Samoyed, chicken, they always make sure they remove all the bones. When Verushka catches the familiar scent of a chicken carcass in the neighbor's garbage can, she devours every bone. The result? One very sick dog. Then there's Charlie Ward who made a game of tossing balls of hamburger to his yellow lab, Quincy; each day he threw the meat higher to see how high the dog could jump. One day the little girl next door threw her new ball in the air; Quincy leaped and swallowed it whole. Another very sick dog!

"How could Quincy possibly confuse a lump of meat with a kid's toy?" Charlie groaned when he saw the vet's bill for surgery to remove the ball. "Don't dogs have a super sense of smell?"

They do, but when they attach companionship and attention to balls of hamburger, their sense of smell gives way to emotions. Besides, the red rubber ball looked a lot like hamburger because it *moved* like a meatball. Just as the touch-induced defense response can override sound and other cues, so the love response can override taste, smell, and even canine common sense.

When owners transfer their food equals something-other-than-food beliefs to their dogs, they can easily close or misdirect rewarding channels of communication and open harmful ones. Medical food-related problems can cause a lot of grief, but behavioral ones can cause even more. Wise owners avoid the problem by not orienting their dogs to food or transferring their own food-related beliefs from the beginning.

We've all seen beauty only in our beholding eyes, and we may even have taken an eye for an eye, or kept an eye on a neighbor's vacant house. In the next chapter we'll discover whether dog and owner can ever see eye to eye.

Optical Illusions

After Ben and Ginny Guptil got their six-week-old rottweiler, Burleigh, from a top kennel, they enjoyed two golden months together. His housetraining progressed smoothly, and the pup followed his owners everywhere.

"Burleigh's so smart," Ginny claimed.

Ben agrees. "We didn't have to train him to stay with us. He just does it. The first dog we had was a mongrel that refused to come when we called. Before her first birthday she got run over by a car and had to be put to sleep. Purebreds are worth the price!"

However, as Burleigh approached five months of age, the Guptils began to wonder. Burleigh no longer stayed close to them on their daily walks. Sure, he still retrieved the bright red Frisbee they tossed across the ball field, but sometimes he would pause to examine other objects, too. Then one day as they passed two teenagers playing Frisbee, the Guptils watched helplessly as their dog dashed off to join the game.

"Burleigh, get back here!" Ben shouted, waving his fist at the departing dog. "Damn dog's just like all the rest."

"I don't understand," groaned Ginny, racing after Burleigh. "He used to be so good; he knows that *blue* Frisbee's not his!"

Seeing Is Believing

My third grade teacher taught me to remember the correct spelling of the word *belief* by saying, "Just remember, there's a 'lie' in the middle of every belief." These words ring especially true in the realm of human perceptions of canine vision. Because vision is such an important means of human communication, we tend to place a great deal of emphasis on it. Have you ever said, "Seeing is believing," or "I'll believe it when I see it with my own eyes"? Apt slogans perhaps, but we'll never see the world as our dogs see it. We have neither the physiological structure, the mental orientation, nor the inherent instincts to see as a dog sees. Whenever I encounter an Irish setter loping along the path, I see a 70-pound, red, silky-coated dog with floppy ears, brown eyes, long legs, and whisking tail; I admire the green bandanna its owner has tied around its neck. But when the setter spots me, he sees an indistinct dull-colored blob making numerous distinct movements. If you add the setter's senses of hearing and smell, he experiences an incredibly smelly, noisy, dull-colored, indistinct moving blob.

Even when owners know their dogs see differently, they often mistakenly treat their pets as if they *can* see as people do. In fact, many owners, generously making allowances for folks with impaired vision or blindness, allow more leeway between other people's vision than they permit between themselves and their dogs. Most of us readily accept that dogs hear and smell better, that is, differently, than people; and our experience, augmented by some reading, confirms species variations in the areas of touch and taste which, although perhaps a bit more difficult to accept, don't require we suspend most personal beliefs. But vision is a sense of a different color. Even though all the physiologists in the world claim our dogs see us as blurry dull blobs whose *motion* makes us distinctive, the majority of us still think our dogs see us as colorful and detailed characters.

Consequently, before we can solve any vision-related problems, we must learn to see as our dogs see. The easiest way to do this is to examine the three main characteristics that distinguish canine from human vision: the following reflex, generalization, and eye contact. Once we understand the dog's point of view, we can apply what we've learned to solve Burleigh's and other sight-related problems.

Monkey See, Monkey Do

In our discussion of sound we learned how dogs mimic, a skill that helps wild pups learn. Visual mimicry serves a similar protective function: when the bitch moves, the pups move. This following reflex or instinctive response to motion, is ten times more sensitive than humans', and enables pups to respond immediately when the need arises. Compare this instinctive reaction with the child's, whose mother must either shout, "Johnny, look out for that truck!" or physically pull the child out of harm's way.

The following instinct persists long after the pups are weaned. As the animal matures and must seek its own food, the instinct to "Follow Mom for safety" gradually begins manifesting itself as "Follow any motion—it could be something to eat!" Thus the original reflex evolves and pups begin to chase moving objects and try to bite them.

How does the following reflex manifest itself in domestic dogs? Remember how the Goodmans taught Ralphie to play tug-of-war by slowly dragging that towel in front of him? They exploited the following reflex. Similarly, owners find young pups like Burleigh stick to them like magnets. Over the years breeders have sharpened the following reflex, creating setters, retrievers, and other bird dogs that respond instantly to objects in flight. The following responses of greyhounds, borzois, and Afghans have been intensified and channeled toward running prey, giving rise to their designation as "sight hounds." Herding dogs such as shelties and collies were similarly developed to take advantage of these breeds' attraction to motion.

If we recognize the dog's tendency to follow anything that moves, we can easily understand why our pets pursue moving objects (that means *any* color Frisbee) or motions we don't even see. To further complicate matters, many owners feel a false sense of security when a young pup transfers its following reflex from its mother to them. Like the Guptils, they appreciate a pup who slavishly follows their every move but can't comprehend why the pup later begins to ignore them. Owners who don't reinforce the mother/owner-centered response quickly see it replaced with the follow-anything-that-moves behavior as the animal matures.

Seeing in General versus Generally Seeing

Assuming any creature can only process so much information at one time, it seems reasonable that sensory systems relying on the collection of a lot of data operate at the expense of other senses. Have you ever concentrated on a book so completely you didn't see someone move your coffee cup? Because canine vision responds so strongly to motion, it shouldn't surprise owners that dogs see less detail and color. If you're being mowed down by a runaway drag racer, you note its speed and direction without worrying about its make and color, two characteristics that might totally absorb you at an auto show.

Although diminished detail and color vision eliminate many visual distractions for predatory animals, it does create problems for household pets, particularly those whose owners believe their dogs see as they do. Imagine a black and white picture of your pen pal's face, with his dark-rimmed glasses, full beard, and ever-present pipe. Now take that mental picture and place it behind a pane of frosted glass. What do you see most clearly? The glasses, the beard, and the pipe.

That's more or less how the dog sees all the time, and it accounts for the dog's reliance on a keen sense of smell to help differentiate the finer details of its environment. Less-than-perfect (by human standards) detail vision leads to the visual phenomenon called generalization. If you had nothing but that blurry photo of your pen pal with which to identify him, chances are you would think every bespectacled, bearded, pipe-smoking male might be he. Dogs react exactly the same way and, depending on the circumstances, the results may be rewarding or alarming.

Suppose you fell in love with your pen pal and longed to meet him. Wouldn't you respond positively to everyone who resembled him? In other words, generalization leads to a consistent positive response over a greater range of incoming data. Dogs who have positive experiences with one meter reader expect them from all meter readers. Those who learn to respond to commands from your kids will probably respond to commands from all children. That's the good news.

The bad news is that generalization can be negatively reinforced, too. A relaxed and confident dog uses all its senses to create a picture of the objects and people in its environment. The senses of hearing and smell help flesh out the more general visual images. When fear accompanies generalized vision, however, alarming behavior may occur. Let's suppose you have a fuzzy picture of someone who threatened your life. Wouldn't you react fearfully and defensively to individuals with the villain's characteristics? The greater the peril you perceive, the more fearfully and defensively you respond. If you feared for your life, you might even mistake your best friend for your antagonist in the dark and respond violently. The same holds true for dogs. If they have an alarming experience with one bearded, bespectacled, or uniformed individual, they feel threatened by them all; only the second time it happens they react defensively by freezing, fighting, or fleeing. However, to the dog-loving paper carrier who replaces the one who threw the evening paper *at* your dog, the dog's unprovoked vicious lunge may seem baffling.

Generalized vision also yields mixed results. For example, the Guptils are pleased when Burleigh recognizes a Frisbee as a plaything; they aren't pleased when he wants to play with someone else's Frisbee. They're thrilled when the young pup follows *them* anywhere; they despair when he wants to follow the neighbor's children to school. A friend of mine labored long and hard to teach his dog to fetch his slippers and loved the dog's enthusiasm for the task. Imagine his chagrin, however, when one wet snowy day he came home to find forty pairs of boots, galoshes, wet shoes, and sneakers on his porch. The dog so enjoyed this form of communication, he'd raided every porch and garage in the crowded housing development to collect "slippers" for his master.

We mentioned how dogs use scent and sound cues to add detail to their generalized visual pictures. If the dog feels confident, it can refine disturbing visual images by using scent or sound. "Yes, this is a bearded image like the one that kicked me, but this one smells different." "Even though that kid moves like the horrible child who stepped on my tail, it doesn't sound like her." However, if the dog lacks confidence or experience, any *single* stimulus can evoke a defensive response. The uniformed, bespectacled, whistling meter reader wearing lemon-scented after-shave who kicks your timid Airedale pup may help create a dog who responds negatively to *all* men, *all* people wearing glasses or uniforms, *all* whistlers, and *all* users of lemon-scented after-shave.

Finding the Face in the Crowd

Eye contact provides one final key to vision-related problems. Just as owners must first orient their dogs if they want them to zero in on voice communication, they must orient them to achieve desired visual communication. Fortunately, we can visually orient a dog the same way we orient another person: by catching its eye. Why bother to establish eye contact? For the same reason we taught our dogs to orient to sound: because we want to establish a common base from which good communication can grow. However, three factors make catching a dog's eye difficult: the placement of the dog's eyes, the dog's increased sensitivity to motion, and the dog's limited detail vision. To some extent, expecting a dog to naturally establish eye contact is like expecting to catch the eye of a particular blue-eyed blonde in a roomful of dancing blue-eyed blondes separated from you by a gauze curtain.

Dogs experience less straight-ahead and more peripheral vision than people because their eyes are usually spaced further apart than human eyes. Because eye contact depends on straight-ahead vision, the placement of canine eyes restricts the opportunity for natural eye contact. This fact, plus the strong canine sensitivity to movement, further frustrate our attempts to catch a dog's eye. Therefore in order to establish eye contact with a dog, we must train it not only to reorient its visual field, but also change its way of seeing things. To achieve eye contact with people, a dog must ignore what it sees best (motion) and pay attention to what it usually ignores (a fixed object).

How can we establish eye contact? Hold your hand level with your dog's nose and slowly move your palm upward toward your face. As the dog follows your motion, its eyes will naturally trail your hand toward your face until you can "catch" and hold its gaze with your own. Repeat this exercise several times daily, following it with a simple command such as "come" or "sit," and lavishing praise for both successful orientation and command response. (Remember, always orient the dog for a reason, to communicate something; otherwise, it will respond for a while, then grow bored.)

Owners can greatly enhance eye contact by simultaneously orienting with sound (and vice versa). The dog who hears the familiar "Come Wolfgang," then immediately turns to look at its owner, pays greater attention than the animal taught to respond to either words or eye contact alone.

When teaching eye contact, never touch your dog in any way. As in the case of sound, touch can override the visual response, so holding the dog's head to make it look at you will often make it try to pull away.

Now that we understand the importance of the following reflex, generalization, and eye contact in canine vision, let's solve some sight-related communication problems.

Creating a New Image for Burleigh

Although the Guptils find it fairly easy to accept Burleigh's running off as normal, they have a harder time accepting their accompanying negative feelings: "I *knew* this would happen. *All* dogs do it." However, Ben and Ginny recognize the value of accepting these feelings *at this time*, and they do wish to communicate effectively with Burleigh. Because they desire a quality relationship with their pet, they begin by considering the Four Basic Options.

"I want to keep Burleigh," Ginny says, "but I can't put up with a dog that takes off all the time."

"I agree," Ben adds. "Our first dog made us nervous wrecks and then having to put her to sleep after she got hit by that car . . . I'd do anything to avoid that."

Having verbalized their willingness to change behavior rather than accept it or get rid of the dog, the Guptils can now define Burleigh's problem. They're surprised that such a seemingly simple one contains so many different components:

Problem	When the Problem Occurs/ Occurred	Possible Explanations
Burleigh doesn't stay close to us or come when we call.	All the time.	He doesn't want to be with us anymore.
		He's found something better to do.
		He doesn't need us anymore.
		He's feeling his oats.
		We've been too lax with him.

He doesn't respond to his Frisbee as much.	All the time.	He's bored with the game.
		There's something more interesting to do.
		He doesn't like his Frisbee.
		He doesn't like playing with us.
He takes off to play with others.	All the time.	He's bored with us.
		The other play excites him more.
		He can't tell the difference.
He chases Frisbees that aren't his.	All the time.	He likes all Frisbees.
		He's responding to something besides Frisbees.
		He can't tell the difference.

Notice how some of the Guptils' answers display strong emotional overtones: We've been *too lax* with him (look out, here comes guilt); He doesn't *like* us (uh-oh, confidence takes a hike); *All* dogs are like that (fear that another dog might fall under the wheels of a car strikes).

The Guptils review the five senses and quickly realize vision plays a major role in Burleigh's unacceptable behavior and that his natural following reflex, lack of detail and color vision, and tendency to generalize have converged to create the problems.

Because Burleigh transferred his following instinct from his mother to them, Ben and Ginny never actually *taught* the pup to stay with them or come when called. As the dog gained experience, he began heeding his emerging "Let's investigate the action" rather than the "Follow me" instinct. The motion of the playing teenagers paralleled his owners' sufficiently to appear nonthreatening, yet was different enough to be intriguing to a curious pup. And of course, Burleigh's limited color vision recognized little difference between the moving red and blue Frisbees.

With this heightened awareness, Ben and Ginny can more easily understand the pup's behavior and embark on a training program to orient him to them rather than just any moving object. First, they teach him to establish eye contact and orient to his name. Then they begin walking him in progressively more distracting areas, all the while holding his attention and praising him for an acceptable response. To take advantage of his following response, they play an indoor game, tying a small weight (washers work well) to the free end of a light rope attached to Burleigh's collar and tossing it back and forth between them. When Ginny throws the washer, Ben simultaneously calls Burleigh, whose natural following instinct stimulates him to follow the washer to Ben, who in turn praises the pup for coming. As Burleigh becomes more proficient, the Guptils make the rope longer and longer and move the training sessions outdoors to areas with more distractions. Eventually they let the rope drag, merely tossing the washer to each other or friends who also call the dog. Finally they abandon the rope entirely, put away the washer and call the dog using only his name, eye contact, and a hand signal mimicking the throwing and catching action.

Because the Guptils train Burleigh consistently and with confidence, the sessions form a solid bond of communication and provide a great deal of fun for all. "It only took three weeks to teach him!" boast the proud owners.

Following and Generalization: The One-Two Punch

Negative effects of the following response in older animals abound, especially when coupled with lack of detail vision. We already saw how Ralphie's innocent tug-of-war game eroded the relationship between him and the Goodmans. Owners of retrievers, setters, or other bird dogs often discover to their horror that their dogs find the neighbor's chickens or parakeets irresistible, whereas sheltie and border collie owners often complain their pets will herd anything that moves, including young children at play. (Sheltie owners can often keep their pets occupied for hours herding each other!) Car, bicycle, and motorcycle chasing also arise from these reflexes, as do chasing and attacking game, including "suburban game" such as other dogs, cats, and even people.

Remember our discussion of taste in Chapter 7 where we noted how dogs use that sense to differentiate "good" prey from "bad"? Of course, we don't want our malamute "tasting" the neighbor's Chihuahua, prized silver Persian cat, or visiting grandson to determine their suitability for his diet. So even though we specifically breed some dogs for a heightened following reflex and a hair-trigger response to motion, we don't want them to carry these instincts to their natural conclusion: the capture and killing of prey. Similarly, although we want the herding breeds to respond to motion with light nips to keep the flock moving, we don't like the problems this inbred behavior can cause in the family pet.

Let's return to our romantic picnicking couple. After Claudia Lehane convinced Mark Stuckey to exchange his boisterous beagle for a delicate sheltie, she again packed her picnic basket with gourmet delights, donned her most alluring frock, and determined that this time no disgusting sniffing hound would spoil the afternoon. The new dog, a female named Violet ("She's so feminine and sweet, just like a little flower!"), behaves like a perfect lady. Just thinking about the mild-mannered dog made Claudia heave a sigh of relief as she spread her blanket once more under the maple in the field of wild flowers; Violet would *never* resort to repulsive scent-hound behaviors.

After nibbling cheese and fruit and sharing a bottle of Beaujolais, Claudia and Mark lay back on the blanket, the waist-high flowers forming a multicolored curtain between them and the rest of the world. Claudia leaned seductively toward Mark, gently stroked his neck, and toyed with the buttons on his shirt.

"What's that?" cried Mark, shooting bolt upright.

"What's what? I don't hear anything." But soon Claudia did hear a sound, like distant thunder rumbling closer and closer.

"My God, Violet's herding a flock of sheep at us! Run!"

When hunting and herding breeds become family pets, all that specialized sight-based behavior doesn't just suddenly disappear. Just because Violet has never seen a sheep in her life doesn't mean she won't find them and their motion intriguing. Just because Quimby, an English setter, lives in a Beverly Hills mansion with bird lover Leslie van Horton doesn't mean the dog's instinct to stalk birds will automatically disappear. As long as Violet orients to motion, all sheep and sheep-sized motion will attract her; and as long as Quimby orients to motion, Ms. van Horton's rare oriental ducks live in constant danger.

Given relatively poor canine detail vision, the only way we can help a dog differentiate objects and people, either visually or with its other senses, is to stop the motion. Once the motion stops, the dog stops. Only then can it orient itself or be oriented some other way, so that "I want to chase and maybe bite this" can be replaced with a more acceptable alternative.

It's not easy, however, when our dogs might suddenly dart into the middle of rush hour traffic to pursue a motorcycle or try to herd a small group of toddlers at a playground; the confidence needed to consistently alter the behavior usually vaporizes. That's why the best method for changing chasing behavior involves setups.

Regardless what the dog chases or herds, the setup follows this basic pattern:

1. First train the dog to orient and respond to the command "sit."
2. Introduce a moving object into the dog's environment at a specific time.
3. Establish eye contact and give the sit command,

holding the dog's attention until the object passes out of sight. Reward the dog for the proper response.

4. If the dog responds to the motion, make sure the subject comes to a screeching halt and freezes, momentarily disorienting the dog.

5. Immediately orient the dog again and repeat the sit command.

6. Once the dog is seated, have the object very slowly move away.

7. Repeat the setup two or three times daily until the negative behavior is extinguished and the dog automatically sits in response to the motion that previously initiated a chase.

Once Mark and Claudia achieve consistent orientation and command responses from Violet, they begin the next phase of the setup. It proved impossible to initially train Violet using sheep for some of the same reasons encountered by many owners whose dogs chase other animals: the owner of the sheep was reluctant to have his animals chased, and there was no way Mark and Claudia could make the sheep freeze the instant Violet started to chase them. (More likely than not, the sheep would run even faster, thereby stimulating the dog to continue the negative behavior, and increasing the chances that one of the animals would be hurt.) Rather than become discouraged, Mark and Claudia began to observe Violet's behavior more carefully, seeking other incidents that evoked the chasing response. Sure enough, they soon discovered that many forms of motion attracted the dog. When Mark tied a cord around a large stuffed animal and slowly dragged it across the living room from a position outside the dog's view, Violet immediately took after it and nipped.

Having created an acceptable decoy, Mark and Claudia were able to continue the training. While Claudia oriented Violet and commanded her to sit, Mark slowly dragged the decoy into the dog's line of vision from his hiding place. If Violet diverted her attention toward the moving toy, Mark stopped the motion immediately and didn't resume it until the sheltie once again oriented and responded to Claudia's command.

Once Violet learned to ignore the toy, Mark and Claudia repeated the orienting and command process in the presence of small animals and children. Eventually they were even able to take the dog to the farm where the sheep were kept and watched proudly as she concentrated on them and their positive response to her new behavior rather than the milling animals.

Of course, using the setup means an owner must find someone willing to donate their Chihuahua, cat, or husband to act as bait, or enlist someone who owns the necessary car, bicycle, or wagon. If your dog might bite, make sure that anyone helping wears heavy clothing, including boots, and that your dog is on a leash and under your control at all times. Don't encourage help from anyone who expresses the slightest discomfort with the training. The inconsistency that results from hesitant or incomplete actions only makes things worse. However, willing and knowledgeable friends can make this sort of training fun.

If your dog chases people, your helper can orient and command the dog to sit after the owner has achieved this response. If the dog chases children, sometimes having a child run with an adult, and repeating the same freeze, orient, and command sequence works nicely. Once the dog responds to the combination, then the pair can run together, but with only the child orienting and commanding the dog. In the final step, the child can run, orient, command, and praise the dog alone. Again, keep the dog leashed and totally under your control during these sessions.

The innate following and generalization response is so strong that consistent setups and enthusiastic praise are critical. Always bear in mind you're asking the dog to ignore a natural means of exploring *its* world because you find that means detrimental and even dangerous in *your* world. Only if you offer something better—your love, praise, and companionship—to replace the following instinct will the dog relinquish it.

Also bear in mind that you're substituting an acceptable behavior that relies on your or some other person's *presence.* Even though your dog responds 100 percent under these circumstances, that's no guarantee it won't revert to its instinctive chase behavior if left to its own devices. So if you know your dog is a chaser, make sure it's confined when you're not there to control it. Not only is this a sign of good interspecies communication, it could save your dog's life and prevent needless harm to your neighbors and/or their property.

The Aging Visionary

As we've seen throughout this book, aging dogs often develop sensory problems. Vision is no exception. The crystal clear lens in the eye of the young animal becomes progressively cloudier with age, complicating the miscommunication canine vision can cause.

Madelyn and Ernie Hobart have had Melbourne, their

Australian Blue Heeler, longer than their ten-year-old son. Melbourne is going on eleven, but he still acts like a young dog; in fact, his owners and their friends often marvel at the dog's apparent agelessness.

One evening while Ernie was sitting in his favorite chair reading the newspaper, Melbourne settled down beside him and stared up lovingly into his face. Ernie looked down at the dog and gasped. "My God, Mel's eyes are cloudy! Do dogs get cataracts? What if he's going blind!"

Madelyn examined the dog. "I never noticed that before. It must have just happened. I'll call the vet tomorrow."

When an aging animal exhibits physiological rather than behavior problems, most owners can accept the condition as normal. However, it usually pays to define the problem so mistaken beliefs don't confuse our interpretation of what we actually see.

Problem	When the Problem Occurs/Occurred	Possible Explanation(s)
Melbourne's eyes are cloudy.	Recently; now, it's always that way.	Normal aging change.
		Eye infection.
		Cataracts.
		Some sort of irritation.
		Cancer.
		Gradual blindness.

Defining the problem helps the Hobarts remain calm. If owners form fixed, but unsubstantiated diagnoses of their older dogs' ailments ("I know he has cancer!" "I'm positive she's blind!"), they subject themselves to fear and all the side-effects fear brings with it. I've seen fear induce temporary deafness in many clients who simply can't or won't hear a word I'm saying. I remember one examination where the owner wailed "Oh God, she's blind" throughout the entire exam, then screamed "Oh thank God, she can see!" when I assured her the dog's eyes were fine. In the meantime, my careful explanation of the animal's true ailment and its treatment fell on deaf ears.

When the Hobarts confront the Four Basic Options, they conclude they certainly don't want to get rid of Melbourne, but they really don't have enough information to decide whether to make any changes. So they take Melbourne to the veterinarian, who tells them that the dog's condition is a common geriatric change called senile dystrophy, in which the lens of the eye becomes cloudy with age.

"How come we just noticed it?" Ernie wants to know.

"Coincidence," replies the vet. "As the change occurs, the dog compensates for the decreased amount of light passing through the lens by opening its pupil wider and using its other senses. Think of a room you want to illuminate using a single window as your light source. To regulate the amount of light, you can open or close the drapes. On bright days you close them more; on overcast days you might need to open them fully. Now suppose your window accumulates a lot of soot and grime. In order to maintain the same amount of light in the room, you must open the drapes more than you did before. Eventually you would open them as much on a sunny day as you used to on a cloudy one; and on gray days you must learn to get along with less light. Melbourne's eyes act the same way. Because his pupil opened more widely than normal to permit entry of the same amount of light, you could finally see the cloudy lens clearly. When Mel was younger you couldn't see the lens because it was clear, and because he kept his pupil closed more in brighter light. So even though the change has occurred gradually, when your reading lamp hit Mel's eyes at the proper angle, it suddenly let you peer into the eye itself."

In response to the Hobarts' concern about their dog's vision, the vet assures them that although their pet can't see as well as he used to, Mel isn't blind. Decreased vision doesn't make a huge difference to an animal whose vision is primarily geared to motion, and motion can become quite fuzzy before a dog loses the ability to perceive it.

What can the Hobarts do to help Melbourne? One option is to begin orienting the dog to scent if they notice him becoming disoriented. Scent works better than sound orientation in older animals whose sense of hearing is more likely to deteriorate with age. Select a *lightly* scented cologne and spray lines of scent approximately 18 inches from the top and bottom step on all staircases, at nose level on that side of the jamb from which doors open, on legs of furniture, and on shoes or ankles when walking the dog. (A light scent is what's needed for a dog's sensitive olfactory system; if the scent is too strong, not only does it irritate both owner and dog, it also confuses the animal.)

Whenever you move furniture or buy new furnishings, spray them so the dog can identify the new location or piece. The dog quickly learns to use the scent, like all forms of orientation, to signal "Pay attention!" and responds accordingly.

After their visit to the vet, the Hobarts, armed with their new knowledge, reconsider the situation. They decide that because Mel acts fine and shows no evidence of vision loss, the best thing to do is to observe him rather than make changes at this time. They set a specific time to reevaluate his condition in three months.

When the Lights Go Out

How well can a dog compensate for a loss of vision with its other senses? I remember examining one old dog whose owners rushed him to the animal hospital in a total panic because he had been "struck blind" at the kennel where he was being boarded. When I examined the dog, I could tell immediately he was quite blind, but I detected none of the signs associated with a *sudden* loss of vision; the dog seemed healthy except for the fact that he kept bumping into things.

"I knew we shouldn't have kenneled him," moaned the guilt-ridden owner. "But we redecorated the house, and Pal gets so upset around strangers."

The redecorating included painting and papering, new flooring, draperies and slipcovers, and rearrangement of furniture. In short, the process had destroyed all the scent cues and predictable placement of furniture the dog had relied on as his vision failed over a period of years. So masterfully had he compensated using scent and touch, his owners didn't notice the blindness until after they had removed his accustomed cues.

Once we identified the problem, the owners willingly returned furniture to original locations, sprayed doorjambs, stairs, and furniture legs with a lightly scented cologne, then reintroduced the dog to his environment. By the end of six weeks, the canine senior citizen could again navigate his household without problems.

Blindness in pups, like deafness, merely requires that owners rely on a different form of communication. Although the owners of deaf animals rely more heavily on visual orientation, owners of blind ones rely more on sound and scent. If the owner of the blind animal accepts the condition as normal and doesn't overprotect the animal, a rewarding relationship can develop. Once the dog develops the confidence that comes from consistent communication, it's no more startled by unfamiliar events than a sighted pet. In fact, some owners of blind dogs feel they're even better pets because they're not plagued by sight-related problems.

Another form of blindness isn't really blindness at all. Often owners of Old English sheepdogs or similarly shaggy breeds let the hair hang over the dog's eyes because they like that particular look. The result? An essentially blind dog to which people react as though it were sighted. If we assume such a dog can see, we don't think to orient it with sound or make our presence known in some other way. Consequently, we're shocked when the dog snaps. A sheepdog who's been smacked on the head or rump by its owner can turn into a shaggy time bomb just waiting to explode at an unsuspecting child; because the dog can barely see, it may perceive even the slightest motion as threatening. It's hard enough for a fully sighted dog to differentiate an upraised arm from one holding the disciplinary rolled-up newspaper. Severely limit its range with untrimmed hair and you can count on trouble.

I remember one sheepdog hospitalized for a hip problem who wouldn't let anyone get near her. As we observed her in a kennel, we noticed that every time she heard a sound she quickly turned toward it and shook her head to momentarily get the hair out of her eyes. Imagine how frustrating and threatening life can be under such circumstances! Fortunately, we were able to build the dog's confidence enough to give her a haircut, and her personality improved immediately.

Have you heard tales of the hazards of cutting the hair over dogs' eyes? The only hazard a haircut causes is a lower score from judges in the show ring. If human show standards dictate that a certain breed should have hair covering its eyes, then anyone who wants to show that breed successfully must let the hair hang over the dog's eyes. Otherwise, trim it for the dog's safety and well-being.

What You See Is What You Get

A final aspect of human versus canine vision is strictly a people problem. Have you ever heard remarks like these?

> "Every time I see a German shepherd or Doberman, I'm terrified. They shouldn't allow dogs like that."
> "I don't know how people can stand those yappy little dogs. I can't even think of them as dogs. They're more like rats."
> "Huskies and malamutes are nothing more than wolves. They've no place in the city."
> "I wouldn't own a white dog on a bet."
> "I'd die before I'd own a long-haired dog."

All of these statements reflect human prejudices based on the physical appearance of various breeds or types of dogs. What do you think the chances are for meaningful communication to occur between each speaker and the object of his or her fear and disapproval? Just as love can overcome the most incredible limitations and open all channels of communication, so prejudice and fear (which are often one and the same) can block those same channels with impenetrable barriers.

If you feel strongly about a particular breed or type and think your prejudices are valid, then you have every right to them, providing you never *have* to communicate with animals you find distasteful. On the other hand, you might find yourself in a predicament similar to Chuck Cranshaw who used to tease his nephew with threats of trapping Yorkshire terriers and Chihuahuas to make stew for his Great Dane. When Chuck fell head over heels in love with a Yorkie-owning commercial artist, he had to reevaluate his beliefs. His lover's Snippet was a well-behaved, gentle, five-pound ball of love and affection who won Chuck's heart in a matter of days. Chuck easily relinquished his prejudice because it had no foundation; he had never known any little dogs before and carried a lot of vague, unsubstantiated ideas about them. As soon as he saw that Snippet didn't fit his stereotype, the prejudice withered and communication blossomed.

Although we humans may possess greater detail vision than canines, we readily succumb to generalized thinking. If we or an acquaintance are frightened or nipped by a shepherd, Doberman, husky, terrier, or miniature poodle, we assume all animals of that breed bite. Slam go the doors, up come the barricades, and communication flies out the window.

Negative incidents occur between or among individuals, not between one person and a breed, group, or species. Many times people bitten by Dobermans are afraid of or dislike all Dobermans, but chances are they had these feelings *before* any negative event occurred. In fact, it's possible that these feelings actually precipitated the event which validated the feelings; I've seen more than one case where a dog responded to a person's fear by biting or other negative behavior.

Just as positive prejudice—i.e., love—enables owners to find new and creative ways to communicate, negative prejudice effectively blocks that communication. To be sure, some owners communicate well with their dogs and *only* their dogs; but to me that's like communicating only with your own kids. It's nice, but there's a lot more communication available for those who have the confidence to seek it out and develop it. If the sight of a certain breed bothers you, analyze your thinking with the six-step process, considering each individual dog and each separate problem. The bad behavior isn't the whole dog, the dog isn't the entire breed, and the breed doesn't represent the entire species.

Now that we understood how all the senses work and how we can use them to communicate with our pet and solve problems, let's look at a very special sense that unites all the senses in a very special way.

Love: The Sixth Sense

Douglas Sitwell gained custody of the family pet, a bois-terous setter named Shawn, after a rigorous court battle with his former wife, Ilene. Having claimed the spoils of victory, Doug soon discovered that the exuberant dog was spoiling his life. Because Ilene had worked at home, Shawn had been totally devoted to her and was used to almost constant companionship. Now the setter had to spend a great deal of time alone and the result was one destructive episode after another.

One evening Doug was greeted by smashed stereo components, overturned shelves, and chewed-up rec-ords and tapes strewn everywhere. In a rage, he grabbed Shawn by the neck and threw him against the wall, frac-turing the terrified dog's leg. Immediately overcome by grief and remorse, Doug rushed the dog to the vet's and the setter was sporting a cast in no time.

"Keep Shawn as quiet as possible," warned the vet. "Put him in a crate or fiberglass kennel when you can't keep an eye on him."

This sounded like such a good idea to Doug he bought a kennel that very day and from then on Shawn was never allowed out except to relieve himself. Although the leg healed beautifully, Doug continued keeping the dog in the kennel and had only the most minimal contact with him. By the time Shawn's former mistress came to see him several months later, the confused dog was an emotional wreck.

"Oh, Doug, how could you!" sobbed Ilene, holding the trembling dog.

Trying to define love as a function of communication is hardly easier than trying to define love itself. Some say all you need is love; others say you can't live on love, that love alone isn't enough. In many ways thinking of love as a sense or vehicle of communication helps clarify its role. Like the other senses, love serves as a medium to carry stimuli or messages from one source to another. Between owner and dog love serves both as an invisible bridge and an invisible leash; it's a pathway that bypasses the limitations of intraspecies communication and permits interspecies interaction. Like a scent, sound, or visual picture, love pictures vary from species to species. Some owners find the way bitches often ignore the weakest in a litter repulsive and barbaric, giving no credence to the idea the bitch's awareness may be far more perceptive than their own. On the other hand, a bitch used to gleaning all sorts of valuable information about her offspring's status as she carefully grooms every inch of them with her sensitive tongue might find our willingness to substitute mere soap and water for this complex process equally incomprehensible. Surely both species could look at each other and say, "How can you *love* your offspring and be involved in behavior like that?"

When a bitch contentedly cleans and nurses her pups, is that love or instinct? A lot of scientists say it's instinct. Many of them also believe interspecies communication can only occur if all species learn to think the same way— which usually means the way we humans do. However, in spite of all that reproducible data saying dogs don't experience love, most dog owners find it ludicrous to even consider it could be any other way. Dog owners (and indeed all pet owners) know they love their pets, and that their pets love them.

Or do they? Although an understanding of love is as critical as that of any sense if we're to develop quality interspecies communication, many owners have difficulty with the reciprocal nature of love. Once we understand the physiology of canine vision, we can accept how our dogs' perceptual world differs from ours without ever entertaining doubts that our pets can indeed see; in other words, unless we or our dogs have some physiological problem affecting vision, we can easily say we know our dogs can see us just as we know we can see them. But when it comes to proclaiming our pet's love for us, few speak with the same certainty with which we declared out four-legged friends' ability to see, smell, hear, or taste. Most of us know how we feel about our pets. The problem is, whether we love our dogs passionately, are mildly ambivalent, or out and out hate them, *we can't be sure how they feel about us*. Sure, Chuck Lepesto knows he'd die for Huggybear, but would Huggybear die for him? Huggy's his best friend in the whole world, but would she stick around if Chuck ran out of dog yummies and the neighbors were barbecuing steaks on their outdoor grill?

Chuck isn't so sure, and neither are most of us. The majority of dogs trained to display such supposedly protective behavior as barking, growling, or snapping are more commonly the result of the owners' attempts to elicit some physical proof of the dog's love and devotion. Even though the owner isn't threatened by the meter reader, paperboy, or motorcycles, the fact that the dog responds defensively to these stimuli is erronously interpreted to mean "I love you. I will protect you." More often than not what the dog is actually communicating is "I'm scared to death!"

When we discussed sound-related problem communication, we said that like begets like, noise begets more noise; and the same holds true for love and confidence. Because owners lack confidence in their dogs' ability and desire to love them, they reinforce protective behavior in their pets that invariably reflects a lack of canine confidence, too.

Playing the Confidence Game

Because we can hardly define love in terms of our own species, is there any way out of this unproductive cycle? Sure there is; if a lack of confidence creates the negative behavior in both owner and dog, then we can rectify the situation by instilling confidence in both.

"That's a joke," says Chuck Lepesto ruefully. "One of the reasons Huggy's my best friend is because I'm so uncomfortable and timid around people!" That's the way a lot of dog owners feel, and there's nothing wrong with this as long as we recognize the effects our lack of confidence has on our dogs. For example, a client of mine always carried a bag of meat scraps in her purse whenever she traveled with her dog, which was most of the time. The dog, a spayed female shepherd mix, was so protective and timid that she went crazy every time her mistress tried to leave the car. The only way the woman could keep from being bitten by the frantic animal was to toss the meat into the backseat of the car and jump out when the dog went to get it.

"Why do you tolerate such behavior?" I asked my client as the dog growled ominously and strained at her leash.

"Because I want the protection."

"But she's not really protecting you; she's scared to death. Someone, including you, could get hurt."

The woman looked me square in the eye. "I was raped once. It's worth it to me to live like this to know no one will ever get that close to me again."

Like begets like. Whatever confidence this young woman once had had obviously disappeared in one dreadful experience. All that remained were her fears, and these were readily communicated to her pet.

Fortunately this story has a happy ending. I saw the woman and her dog about two years later and the change in both was remarkable. Both moved easily and confidently, all traces of the fear-based rigidity and tension gone. I was burning to know what great miracle had changed their attitudes so dramatically. The miracle was a six foot two, two-hundred pound ex-marine spouse. When love comes in, confidence invariably follows, leaving no place for fear.

If there aren't any ex-marines around to build confidence in you and your dog, you can do it yourself. Begin teaching your pet simple commands in the calm environment of your home, then gradually move your training sessions into more and more distracting and populated areas. Shopping centers and city parks are fine for this sort of confidence building. As your confidence grows, it will no longer seem so unlikely that your dog likes being with you and loves you just as you love it.

What Difference Does It Make?

We already know we can effectively communicate with our dogs using all sorts of sense data, so what difference does it make whether we love our dogs or believe they love us? To me, it's the difference between a good relationship and a great one. It's also the difference between a relationship based on what each participant *does* versus what each *is*. Perhaps this sounds too abstract to be practical, but what other reason could explain the plethora of incredible dog stories that span all ages and civilizations? Why are there always dogs risking their lives to save humans and vice versa? Why are we always hearing stories of dogs like Bobbie who traveled over two thousand miles in six months to be reunited with his family? What magic enables Barbara Woodhouse to train as many as eighty dogs in one day?

The answer, despite all the scientific data that may on the surface appear to the contrary, must have something to do with love. Is it magic? Only to those who don't have the confidence to experience it for themselves.

That Old Black Magic

In spite of the romantic ballad, nothing is blacker than love gone wrong. Although we recognize that people change and relationships evolve, we tend to think those we have with our pets are fixed and unchanging. In fact, many owners point to their dogs' constant and unchanging nature as their pets' most appealing quality, thereby setting the stage for possible miscommunication. Let's add this quality of change to a relationship and see how the Sitwells' misinterpretation of love created problems for themselves and their dog.

Because Shawn was home all day with Ilene, the setter naturally developed a stronger bond with her, which his mistress readily reinforced. When Doug and Ilene's own relationship began to falter, Ilene turned more and more of her attention to the dog, and although the dog was most assuredly a great comfort to Ilene during this troubled time, this shift in attention also contributed to two other changes: it increased Shawn's attachment to, and dependency on, Ilene, and it made Doug resent a previously loved pet.

Just we often project our beliefs and fears on our dogs, so we often make them symbols in our interactions with other people. Certain breeds become symbols of our wealth and social status, whereas others are believed to confer a more masculine or feminine image upon their owners. In the Sitwells case, Shawn became the symbol of who "won" the divorce and who "won" the dog's love; only, as is often the case, the symbol didn't live up to its meaning in real life. What Doug viewed as a well-behaved companion turned out to be an unruly and destructive pain in the neck. The shattered dream of yet another relationship gone wrong was more than he could bear, and he took his frustrations out on the dog.

Several times throughout our discussion, I've recommended denning as a most effective and sensitive training technique. However, as we see here, even the best method can go awry if the proper channels of communication aren't functioning. In theory, denning Shawn makes sense for medical and behavioral reasons; but because Doug did it more to punish the dog than out of his love and concern for Shawn, the results were devastating.

This is one of those sad cases that doesn't really have an ending. Does Doug Sitwell love his dog? Ilene implies in her accusatory question he can't possibly, but I'm not so sure. If love is a sense, or rather a sensory link or leash, I suppose one could lose it temporarily the same way one could lose one's sense of hearing or sight. But if a person has known love as Doug did indeed at one time with Shawn, is there any way he can forget?

When love isn't present in a relationship for whatever reason, its effects are far more devastating than a deficit in or lack of one of the other senses. I think the difference between a love deficit and a deficit of hearing, vision, taste, smell, or touch is the difference between the collapse of a bridge and the breakdown of one car on that bridge. If the love isn't there, all forms of communication are negatively effected. If love is present, even the most extraordinary and bizarre forms of communication can succeed.

Too Much of a Good Thing

Is it possible to love our pets too much? I don't think so. I think a lot of pet owners who view themselves or others that way confuse love with infatuation. Remember: love is quiet and gentle, love is not arrogant or rude. People who feel they must constantly display affection for their dogs or remind others of their dogs' love for them are usually those who have the least confidence in that love. Owners who have confidence in their relationship with their pets don't have to boast about or defend them. This doesn't mean they don't care about their relationships; it just means that they're free to rely on intuitive rather than conscious recognition.

Love isn't a thing, an end in and of itself. It's a communicating link, an energy source that enables us to tap into others and create new and wondrous experiences. In our final chapter we'll examine some more pragmatic uses for this unifying component of our invisible leash.

Making the Ultimate Connection

The Eberhards' two purebred dogs have been raised with children, rock music, erratic comings and goings, car rides, and much varied experience with the family. Every visitor is greeted like a long lost friend, and the dogs sleep in their owners' beds or on the couch. They're outside only long enough to relieve themselves or participate in family activities. Although they're perfectly behaved most of the time, both dogs will soil in the house, chew and dig destructively, and bark when left alone. In spite of these vices, the Eberhards love their dogs, and the animals are immediate favorites of any dog-loving visitors in their home.

About ten miles away from the Eberhards', the Comiskys share their household with mixed breed male and female littermates who live outdoors most of the time.

One dog, usually the female, is permitted to run loose, whereas the other is chained to the doghouse; if both animals are free at the same time, they take off into the woods and are gone for hours. Both dogs are very shy and the male has been known to snap. Although the dogs occasionally enter the house, they seldom remain indoors for very long. For the most part, these animals spend their entire lives in the immediate vicinity of the house and have little contact with other animals or people. Whenever a strange vehicle or person enters the Comiskys' property, the dogs growl and bark defensively. If a visitor attempts to make friends with the animals, they either try to run away, freeze, or snap.

In this chapter we're going to put all we've learned together and look at some other common problems. Now that we know how the various senses contribute to problems and their resolutions individually, let's see how the final sense, love, helps us unravel even the most complex multiple ones. Although we may argue about the severity of the problems exhibited by the animals in our two households and even make judgments about the personalities of the humans involved, the fact remains that these behavioral potpourris aren't particularly uncommon.

The Eberhard dogs exhibit the following problems: destructive chewing and digging, house soiling, and barking. In the Comisky household, the dogs' problems are equally varied: growling, snapping, and excessive shyness. It's easy to see that virtually every sense is involved in each problem. So where do we begin? The starting point is always the same: the Four Basic Options. But in cases where multiple problems are present, I like to preface evaluation of the four options with one more consideration: How do you feel about the dog?

Using the Invisible Leash

When we began our discussion of communication, we said love and confidence go hand in hand for dog and owner alike, and a willingness to change or accept the existing conditions without negative feelings results from that love and confidence. If the love and confidence for self and pet aren't present, the commitment necessary to change problem behavior or learn to live peacefully with it can't be there, either. If Gretchen Eberhard views her year-old Pekinese as a poor substitute for her now deceased show quality Bedlington terrier, her chances of solving the former's problems are about nil. In fact, it's quite possible that Gretchen's attitude is a *cause* of the dog's problems as well as a hindrance to their resolution.

When solving all problems, but particularly when solving multiple ones, love and the resultant confidence and commitment must be unflappable. Love is the widest channel and purest form of communication. As long as we can look Bozo square in the eye and say "I know you love me and I know I love you and that love isn't lessened by the mess on the rug, garbage spread all over the kitchen floor, the six-foot deep hole dug in the peonies, the summons from the dog officer, or threats from the neighbor," we can solve anything. Sound simple? Try it. Imagine yourself confronting your dog and a favorite skirt with a horrible urine stain, a treasured book chewed to shreds, or a prized flower garden reduced to pathetic stubble. Imagine your feelings about the dog and yourself at that instant. If you're like most owners, you'll be angry and disappointed in the dog, and feel frustrated and inadequate yourself. Now imagine how you respond. Here again the responses of most owners are fairly typical. If this is a first offense, owners usually respond with some sort of punishment, followed by forgiveness. A second infraction usually results in more punishment and less forgiveness because it implies two additional negative behaviors: the failure of the dog to learn from the first experience, and the failure of the owner to properly train the dog. If the behavior is a repeated offense, usually by the third infraction the dog/owner relationship is living on borrowed time.

Imagine your scenario as a first, second, and tenth offense and see how your feelings and responses are altered. Don't think in terms of a "right" response or what you *should* feel or do; merely become aware of how you *normally* respond. Sound familiar? Whether we're dealing with single or multiple problems, step one is always the same: define the existing behavior and our responses to it as normal.

Now that you recognize your normal pattern of response to your pet's negative behavior, let's do that same exercise again—only this time begin by taking a deep breath, establishing eye contact with the errant beast, and saying: "I know I love you and you love me and that can't be lessened by anything either one of us may do." Although this sounds so simple, it's extremely difficult for many owners to accomplish; and it's often their frustration at their failure to do so that leads to any physical punishment rather than the negative behavior itself.

"That's foolish," says Ms. Eberhard. "We know we love our dogs." That's true for most owners; but a lot of us don't have the confidence in that love to believe it takes precedence over our sloppy inconsistent training and capricious disciplining, or our dogs' destructive chewing and digging. We adore our dogs because they continue showing affection even when we've responded to them as complete irresponsible fools. We're repulsed by our pets when they show that *same* affection when they've committed something we consider horrible. Dogs willingly and naturally forgive *and* forget if the love bond is strong, whereas we humans tend to spend so much time agonizing over forgiveness that forgetting often becomes impossible. In such cases, we'd be far better off to mimic our dogs' short attention spans and concentrate on forgetting the incident, leaving the forgiveness to take care of itself.

Mirror, Mirror

A technique that's extremely helpful when developing confidence in our ability to communicate with our dogs is to imagine a mirror superimposed over the dog's face such that we can see ourselves as well as the dog whenever communication occurs. The mirror keeps us honest, and enables us to sense immediately if what we're communicating to our pets is inconsistent with our beliefs about the pets—and ourselves. By using this technique we're constantly reminded that communication between dog and owner is really a four-way street:

- the message we send the dog
- the message the dog receives from us
- the message the dog sends to us
- the message we receive from the dog

Although we like to believe there's perfect agreement among all these channels, the mirror reminds us this is often not the case. Even if through our knowledge of our dog's perceptual differences we learn to make the necessary adjustments in our human transmissions so our dogs receive the messages we want them to, their interpretations will never be exactly the same as ours.

When John Comisky screams at his dog—"Don't you know these people are friends!"—the mirror quickly tells him that his interpretation of the visitors' status isn't the same as that of his pet. The mirror technique takes some practice, but it makes the exchange of sense data flow much more smoothly.

The Big Picture

Once we have confidence in our feelings about our dogs and our relationships, accept the existing conditions as normal, and decide some changes would improve things, we're ready to define the problem. Rather than work through each problem separately, view them altogether as part of an integrated unit and look for common or unifying threads. For example, when the Eberhards examine their list of problem behaviors, they discover that the majority of them occur when the dogs are left alone. On the other hand, the Comisky dogs tend to exhibit their most negative behavior in response to other people.

The pattern exhibited by the Eberhard pets is by far the more common. Because dogs are social, territorial, and curious by nature, being left alone or isolated creates a great deal of tension for most canines; in fact, some behaviorists estimate that as much as 90 percent of *all* negative behavior in dogs is related to isolation. Depending on the dog's personality, this behavior may take many different forms. More extroverted dogs may bite or chew furnishings and dig holes, whereas more introverted ones may suck holes in clothing or lick and scratch themselves to the point of creating disfiguring sores. The extroverts bark and howl in response to each passerby, siren, or other novel stimuli; introverts bark and howl for no apparent reason and often whine between bouts of the former. Extroverts isolated outdoors try to take off; introverts try to get back into the house. Both types of animals resort to house-soiling, primarily as a means of marking their territory.

Although the Comisky dogs are by nature social animals, their environment and introverted personalities have limited the development of their social skills toward people because the Comiskys lead very quiet lives and seldom have visitors. Although there is a very strong bond between owners and dogs, it doesn't carry over to other people.

"How come?" asks Gina Comisky. "I thought that the dogs' generalized vision would make them love all people the way they love us." It would—if we were just dealing with a problem of visual communication; but this is a problem involving all the senses, including love and confidence. When dogs are kept in limited environments like the Comiskys', the more introverted ones become shyer and shyer. Eventually this shyness leads to a sense of vulnerability which may eventually manifest itself in defensive behavior—freezing, fleeing, or fighting.

Using this broader view of multiple-problem situations, we can define both the Eberhards' and the Comiskys' problems as primarily the result of isolation. In the Eberhards' case, the normally extroverted, highly socialized, and people-oriented dogs exhibit their worst behavior when left alone. The Comisky dogs' isolated life-style has left these more introverted animals poorly socialized, and they exhibit their worst behavior in the presence of what they consider unnatural human company.

Finding the Answers

Listing all the possible solutions for all the problems could overwhelm even the most loving and dedicated owner. However, because we've found the underlying cause that often creates multiple dilemmas, we can concentrate on that cause. In both of our examples, we know isolation to one degree or another is a major factor: the Eberhard dogs don't like it, the Comiskys do.

One obvious solution is for the owners to give the dogs what they want: the Eberhards could rearrange their lifestyles so the dogs are never alone, and the Comiskys could make sure no visitors ever came to their home. However, although some owners' confidence in their relationship with their dogs is so minimal they will totally rearrange their lives to circumvent some negative behavior, these results are tenuous at best. Because the owner is responding to subtle or blatant intimidation, or so he or she believes, they eventually come to resent the dog and view it as a canine albatross hung about their necks. Even the most timid owner invariably has a difficult time justifying and maintaining a relationship based on one-sided guilt and martyrdom.

Even though most owners find it impossible to alter all of the environmental conditions that normally contribute to negative behavior, few wish to tolerate the existing behavior, either. The next step, then, is to examine some possible solutions somewhere between these two extremes. Many times when dogs exhibit isolation behavior we feel the only true solution is the exact opposite: total freedom. However, we often overlook the other possible solution: more confinement.

Think back to what we said about dogs' perceptual abilities—their increased hearing, sensitivity to motion and odors, response to touch—in terms of their territorial behavior. Although some behavioralists may attribute territoriality to strictly physiological and instinctive functions, I believe this behavior is intimately related to love. The tighter the bond between owner and pet, the stronger the animal's feelings for the owner and his or her property. When the Eberhard dogs are locked in the house unable to either patrol their domain or explore novel stimuli, they're frustrated. When visitors intrude, the Comisky dogs feel bound to protect their owners' property even though all their other instincts are telling them to run. In both cases sensory data floods the dogs and a common message comes through loud and clear: "Find out what that noise, person, smell, or motion is. Protect your territory." Only the Eberhard dogs can't, and the Comisky dogs don't want to.

Owners sensitive to similar dilemmas can remove a great deal of the tension and eliminate much of the negative behavior simply by restraining their dogs. Denning nicely resolves much of the tension-induced barking, chewing, digging, and house-soiling behavior occurring in animals confined indoors. Dogs exhibiting such behavior outdoors may also be denned, but the kennel or crate should be placed indoors. The idea is not only to create a safe haven for the dog, but also to eliminate as much tension-producing inaccessible stimuli as possible. Aside from the obvious dangers inherent in climate control (too hot in summer, too cold in winter), denning a dog at the end of the driveway where it's still assaulted by all those real or imagined territorial threats hardly decreases tension or frustration. Under such circumstances, the dog who used to chew on the door may simply start chewing on itself instead.

Place the den in a secluded spot, preferably in a favorite person's bedroom or in the laundry room next to a basket of dirty clothing where the dog will be surrounded by familiar scents. Owners who normally listen to the radio find leaving it on in their absence helps calm the dog, serving as an audible reminder of the owner as well as blocking out possible threatening sound stimuli. However, only use the radio if it's part of your normal routine. One elderly client who led a very quiet life with her dainty pug was told to leave a radio on for her pet, but because the dog wasn't used to it, the sound of music and strange voices in the house drove the poor animal to distraction—destructive distraction.

Like denning, owners often view any form of restraint including leashes a violation of the dog's freedom and a negative judgment against their ability to train a dog. The measure of true freedom is confidence. An animal who's terrified of the territorial implications of protecting fifty acres is far more imprisoned by its instincts and lack of confidence than the dog chained contently to its house or sleeping in its crate. Freedom isn't a matter of where you are; it's a matter of how you feel. As in our evaluations of love, confidence, and punishment relative to our dogs, it's extremely valuable to put the mirror up when we explore our beliefs about freedom.

Not only does some form of restraint remove a great deal of tension from the timid (and consequently, usually overly protective) animal, it's also our moral obligation. For some reason many owners have difficulty accepting a most simple and basic truth: we are responsible for our dogs' behavior, *without exception*. The law expects us to know our pets and be able to communicate with them at all times. Notice the law doesn't expect our dogs to be well-mannered. The law doesn't care whether your dog rips your house to shreds or turns your yard into a mine field as long as it doesn't bother anyone else or their property. However, if your dog does anything that's considered dangerous or a nuisance—including running out in front of cars as well as nipping meter readers—regardless of the circumstances, you're responsible. If your pet exhibits any such behavior, make sure you use a reliable means of restraint, even if you plan to initiate a program of training to eliminate the behavior. When the animal isn't under your *total* control via verbal or some other form of communication, use mechanical restraint. Your dog and your neighbors will thank you.

A Little Knowledge Goes a Long Way

Once the Eberhards and Comiskys initiate denning and restraint as an immediate solution to end the destruction and possible threat to others, they begin collecting more specific information. Both families learn their dogs' wide range of behavioral problems spring from the animals' relative lack of confidence and, as we already know, nothing builds confidence like learning.

Because the Eberhards and their growing family live in a populated area, they decide to spend the necessary time training their dogs. "If the dogs can't handle the stress now," reasons Les Eberhard, "it's only going to get harder for them as they get older." Les is totally correct; in fact, many timid dogs that start out exhibiting only isolation barking, chewing, digging, and house-soiling often resort to more defensive biting or snapping later. The Eberhards enroll the dogs in a ten-week obedience course and initiate a daily program of training involving all family members. Coupled with denning, this confidence-building regime pays off in a matter of months. Although the Eberhards never specifically train the dogs not to bark, dig, chew, or soil in the house, by removing the tension of isolation via denning and building their pets' confidence through training, these frustration-based behaviors simultaneously disappear.

To be sure, the Eberhards could extinguish the negative behavior by using setups like the Hanffs in Chapter Four or Mark and Claudia in Chapter Six. However, in the case of behavior related to isolation and lack of confidence, setups treat only the symptoms and not the cause. The Eberhards may stop the frustrated barking, chewing, or digging using setups, but more often than not, such practices only add to the turbulent sea of apprehension boiling within the pet. Eventually, the frustrations rise and manifest again, usually in a more detrimental or destructive form.

The Comiskys take a completely different approach to their dogs' behavior. Rather than embark on a program of confidence building socialization, they opt simply to restrain the animals. Although the Eberhards might consider this irresponsible owner behavior, let's listen to the Comiskys' reasons:

"We talked to several behaviorists and trainers who said that, in order to properly socialize the dogs, we'd have to use daily setups as well as training sessions. Because the dogs are afraid of strange people and vehicles, those elements would have to be incorporated into the training; in other words, we'd have to commit ourselves to a program involving the very things we retired to the woods to get away from. Frankly, it's not worth it to us. The dogs are old and so are we. In spite of all our attempts to get them to spend more time indoors with us, they prefer the outdoors and don't mind being tied."

In this case the Comiskys express their love and confidence in their relationship with their pets in a completely different way. Because their lifestyle is such that the negative behavior manifests only occasionally, they feel they can *accept* that behavior without feeling guilty or altering their positive relationship with their dogs. Because they're confident in their ability to communicate with their pets, they're secure in their belief that the dogs don't mind being restrained. Obviously, if either John or Gina found the idea of tying the dogs distasteful or believed the dogs resented it, this type of solution would never work.

In both cases, we see how multiple problems can be quickly reduced to a single underlying cause which owners can then resolve according to the interpretation of collected information and their own needs. As long as love and a sense of commitment are present from the beginning, a solution is always found.

One Problem at a Time

Another way of viewing multiple communication problems is piecemeal. Like different breeds of dogs have different stimulus sensitivities, so different owners often react more strongly to some problems than others. For example, the Eberhards have five active sons ranging in age from eleven to nineteen and, consequently, their normal life-style includes a lot of noise and more than one dented, mended, or otherwise less-than-perfect piece of furniture. Because of this, the dogs' barking, chewing, and digging don't really bother Gretchen Eberhard. However, although her household may be a little shop- or child-worn in appearance, Gretchen prides herself in its cleanliness, and the mere idea of urine and stool in the house totally repulses her. So whether all the existing problems have the same underlying cause or not, house-soiling is the only one that concerns Gretchen, and it's the one she concentrates on.

Similarly, the Comiskys can easily tolerate canine be-havior that reflects their own reclusive life-style. How-ever, one cherished visitor is their beloved granddaugh-ter, and Gina and John would die if the dogs threatened or harmed the child in any way. Therefore it's worth it to them to drive 30 miles daily to pick up the child, bring her to their home, and gradually accustom the dogs to her presence, helping both dog and child develop love and confidence in each other. Although this is a tedious process, it's a labor of love for the Comiskys and more than worth the effort.

The major disadvantage of piecemeal problem solving is that it often complicates the process unnecessarily. By the time Gretchen solves her dogs' house-soiling prob-lem, she could have solved all their problems. In the time it takes the Comiskys to socialize their dogs to their granddaughter they could have socialized the animals to all people. However, if owners truly believe that there's only one problem, regardless how narrowly defined it is, that's invariably the only one they concentrate on. One client's puli chewed shoes with a vengeance when-ever left alone, but his owners' only concern was keeping the dog from destroying one particular pair. I suggested denning to relieve the isolation anxiety leading to the chewing, but this was immediately dismissed as being "too cruel." "Why don't you put the shoes where the dog can't reach them?" was my second suggestion.

"Doctor, you don't seem to understand. Pierre can chew any of my shoes he wants except that pair. I think I'm being more than fair and the least he can do is respect my feelings."

In this case, setups were used to eliminate the problem; but like so many piecemeal solutions, the underlying miscommunication between owner and pet continued.

Following Up: The Finishing Touch

Sometimes it's difficult to determine whether we're solving the whole problem or just part of it until we evaluate our results. If we know we have multiple problems to begin with, this evaluation becomes even more critical. For example, the Eberhard dogs showed great improvement at the end of their second and third months of training, but marked deterioration by the end of the fourth. At that time, the Eberhards discovered their sons had become quite lax about the training and the dogs were resorting to their old behavior patterns again. Although everyone had a clear understanding of what the dogs' problems were and how to resolve them, the evaluation pointed out that there were people problems to be attended to also. An open and frank family discussion revealed that the two older boys resented the daily training sessions but felt guilty about expressing this to the rest of the family; instead, they spent less and less time with the dogs. Fortunately, once the problem was known, the younger children and parents were willing to take up the slack without making the others feel negligent or less caring about the pets. Although this dog problem had become a people problem, using the power of the sixth sense—love—helped overcome it.

What if the Eberhards can't agree on a solution that's acceptable to all? That's a tough question to answer. We all like to believe we're able to compromise, but in truth, compromise only works if our beliefs aren't very strong to begin with. If our ideas are strong, compromise for more than a short period only leads to greater resentment, then anger, then guilt. What begins as a dog-human communication problem becomes full-blown human emotional chaos. Unless it's felt that a short-term compromise for a *specific* time period with a highly defined goal is tolerable to all involved, it's far better to learn to live with the dog's negative behavior.

During one of the Comiskys' periodic evaluations of their dogs, they realize the female is becoming even more upset by the presence of strange vehicles or people. A trip to the vet's for a complete physical reveals the dog suffers from a congenital hip problem. The resulting discomfort makes the dog feel even more vulnerable than usual, thereby increasing her defensiveness. When she ran loose most of the time, her exercise schedule was consistent and her hips didn't bother her; now that she's restrained, she's not able to compensate as well. The veterinarian suggests that the Comiskys initiate regular daily walks for the dog as well as medication, and she soon resumes her normal pattern of behavior.

Had these owners not routinely evaluated their dogs' progress, they would have missed these important changes.

The Ultimate Connection

Throughout this book we've repeatedly referred directly and indirectly to love as a critical factor in the total communication forming an invisible leash between owner and dog. Unfortunately, many owners have some fairly rigid ideas about what leashes are supposed to do. "They keep the dog from running away," says Gretchen Eberhard. "Leashes keep dogs from getting into trouble," adds John Comisky. "It's a way to control them." These statements reflect common views that a leash is a mechanical means of displaying our dominance or control over our animals; a leash is our insurance that our dogs won't leave us and that they'll do what we want them to do. What few people realize is that, regardless who or what is at either end of the leash, *both* participants are equally bound and limited by its presence. The owners whose dogs drag them down the street are no freer to experience their normal means of locomotion than their dogs, and owners who maintain control by virtue of leashes alone know they have absolutely no control if they're not at the other end of those leashes.

However, now we know there's a much less restrictive way to view a leash. We now know that a leash can also serve as a bridge, a physical communication link between owner and pet much like a toddler hanging onto a mother's skirt or two lovers huddling beneath a blanket. Suddenly, our symbol of limited freedom and servitude becomes one of comfort, communication, and love.

I don't think there's a dog owner alive who wouldn't want the security of a leash without the restrictions of its physical presence. We all have visions of walking through the most populated cities or rugged woodlands with our dogs at our sides, not slavishly devoted or fearfully attentive, but relaxed and comfortable, sometimes making a brief side trip just as we stop to look in a shop window or follow the flight of a hawk. When our dream dog momentarily leaves our sides we don't panic; we know it'll be all right and will always return. It doesn't have to stay two paces behind our left heel or sit when we sit; we know it can and will willingly do these things if we ask, but it's rarely necessary. Sometimes we think our dream dog has been gone too long, but just about the time we're getting ready to whistle or call, it comes. Maybe we say something welcoming the dog, maybe we don't. Maybe all we do is share that very special look and feeling.

Even though your dog's behavior may be quite different from the behavior of the dog just described, if you're like me, your dog *is* your dream dog. So maybe your dog is an unruly fuzzball you suspect would hightail it for greener pastures the instant you turned your back. Does this mean you're a failure and poor communicator? Not in the least—it means exactly the opposite. The fact that you can envision yourself sharing this special relationship that transcends simple obedience and defies verbalization with that unruly fuzzball tells you the invisible leash, the bond of love, is already in place. All you have to do is learn to trust it—and yourself—and use it.

Perhaps we ought to be able to trust that bond intuitively, like the stray dog with the broken leg who showed up on the orthopedic surgeon's front porch or the lost hiker who trusted his 8-pound Pomeranian to lead him to safety; but most of us don't have that much confidence in ourselves or our dogs. We have to work at it; we have to create ways to prove that the love is there. Some of us feel getting the dog to respond instantly to our commands is sufficient proof; others feel the dog's willingness to accept symbolic gifts of food, special sleeping quarters, or apparel with the same response as another human indicates the bond is present. However, the wisest owners fortify their confidence in the power of the invisible leash via knowledge: The more we know, the more confidence we have, and the more we have to share with others regardless of species. I suspect the reason some have difficulty communicating is because they've never taken the time to learn about or from their pets; consequently, they have nothing in common to communicate.

The value of love as the invisible leash bridging the gap between owner and dog and permitting the free flow of all forms of communication was brought home to me quite clearly by my son. I was involved in one of my typical exchanges with one of my dogs: "Dacron, you crazy old dog, you're the best dog in the whole world!"

"Oh, Mom," groaned my son. "You say that to all the dogs!"

He's right, I do—and I always mean it, too. When open interspecies communication exists, every dog is the best dog in the whole world. When I cradle my dog's head in my hands and look deep into his eyes, beyond his sleeping in my flower beds, and past my own inconsistent and distorted reflection, what do I see? I see what all dog owners who take the time and have the confidence to totally communicate with their pets see. Beyond that distorted reflection and jumble of scents and sounds, beyond those highly unique sensations sent and received, is an ever-present, durable, highly flexible, and not the least bit restraining bond called love. To be bonded to another isn't bondage at all: it's total freedom and the purest form of freedom. The bond is already in place, ready to go; all we have to do is learn to recognize it.

Take a long deep look at your dog and what do you see? At first you may see only a reflection of your own beliefs, but take all you've learned about interspecies communication and look again. There; now you know what your dog knew all along. You're the best person, the best companion for the best dog in the world.

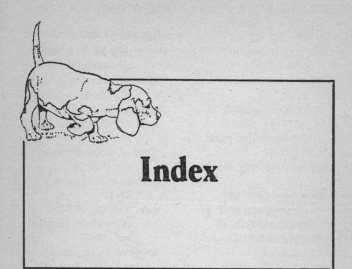

Index

Index